HOW TO BE A CHILLI HEAD

HOW TO BE A CHILLI HEAD

INSIDE THE RED-HOT WORLD OF THE CHILLI CULT

BY
ANDY LYNES

PORTICO

CONTENTS

WELCOME TO THE WORLD OF

They say some like it hot. These days, when it comes to food, you can replace 'some' with 'just about everyone'. The world has gone chilli crazy, from the dazzling array of bottled sauces on the supermarket shelves to piri piri chicken and burritos in high street restaurants.

However, no one likes it hotter than Chilli Heads, that passionate and quite possibly deranged band of heat-seeking chilli-philes who won't look at a bottle of sauce unless it has a skull and crossbones and the words 'approach with caution' on it, and don't get out of bed for less than five figures in Scoville units.

But what does it take to become a Chilli Head? What exactly do they do, what sets them apart from the rest of the chilli-loving world, and where do they live? This book sets out to answer all these questions and more.

THE CHILLI HEAD

How To Be A Chilli Head takes you inside the red hot chilli cult and tells you everything you need to know about how to grow chillies, how to form your own Chilli Head club, where the best chilli festivals in the world are, how to market your own sauce and launch your own Chilli Head internet channel.

Being a Chilli Head makes you part of a worldwide movement of people. A strange worldwide movement, admittedly, but one that knows how to push the boundaries and have The Most Fun while doing it. So, Chilli Heads of the world, it's getting hot in here, let's take off all our clothes... (no, hold on, that's a whole different book). Chilli Heads, for those about to feel the burn, we salute you!

1

THE ESSENTIAL KNOWLEDGE

CULT OF THE CHILLI HEAD

(OR, HOW THE HUMBLE CHILLI BECAME A FOOD-WORLD SUPERSTAR)

Rock stars have their groupies, film stars have their fans but fruit just has its consumers. Except for chillies, that is (yes, chillies are a fruit, actually berries, and not a vegetable because they contain seeds). Chilli Heads are more committed than the most fervent Belieber, more devoted than one of Lady Gaga's Little Monsters and more insane than a Tom Cruise stalker. Well, no one's that crazy, but you get the idea.

Although chillies have been cultivated and appreciated for thousands of years, the cult of the Chilli Head is a modern phenomenon. The origins of the term Chilli Head have been obscured by history, but it was most likely coined sometime after 1946, when the Chili (US spelling!) Appreciation Society (now the Chili Appreciation Society International) was formed in Dallas to 'improve the quality of chilli in restaurants and broadcast Texas-style recipes all over the earth'. Founder George Haddaway was referred to as 'Chief Chili Head' in the press and, as the society grew in America and around the world, the name stuck.

Back then, George and his chums were mostly concerned with making sure people cooked chilli con carne the Texas way, but now being a Chilli Head is a much more complex affair. It's not just about the food on the plate but the culture that's grown up around the planet's most thrilling fruit. (Ever got excited about an apple? Didn't think so).

The Chilli Head phenomenon is really only found in cultures where hot food doesn't form the mainstay of the cuisine, mostly concentrated in Europe, North America and Australia. Chillies are so central to the cuisines of Thailand, Malaysia, Mexico, China and India, for example, that to single out part of the population as 'Chilli Heads' would be nonsensical.

Modern Chilli Head culture can be traced back to events in America in the late 1980s, including the opening of Le Saucier in Boston, Massachusetts, the first ever chilli sauce store, the creation of the super-hot Blair's Death Sauce and in 1994, the cultivation of the Red Savina, the first super-hot fresh chilli.

The shared love of 'fiery foods' in real life at festivals and conventions, and later online in forums and via video reviews, has fuelled the growth of the cult exponentially. Chillies now take their place alongside a very select band of foods, such as caviar, white truffles and Wagyu beef, that are capable of creating genuine excitement. But, unlike those other gourmet items, you don't have to be a millionaire to appreciate them. That's really something worth getting hot under the collar about.

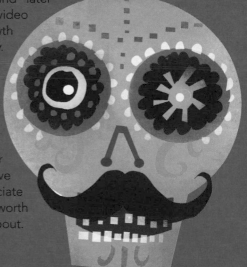

CHILLI TIMELINE

7,000 BC
Evidence of wild chillies being gathered in Mexico.

3,400 BC
Chillies cultivated in Mexico.

900
Pueblo tribes grow chillies in Southwest of America. Chillies become central to Incan, Mayan and Aztec cuisines.

1966
A Bowl of Red by Frank X. Tolbert published.

1947
Dave Pace founds the Pace Food Company in Texas and sells first bottle of Picante sauce made with jalapeños, onions and tomatoes.

1946
George Haddaway and Jim Fuller co-found the Chili Appreciation Society.

1912
Wilbur Scoville invents the Scoville scale.

1967
First chilli cook-off held in Terlingua, Texas.

1975
Larry Levine opens the first Chili's Grill & Bar restaurant in a converted postal station in the Vickery Meadows area of Dallas, Texas. There are now 1,500 Chili's Grill & Bars around the world.

2012
The Carolina Reaper chilli takes the hottest chilli crown with more than 2 million SHU

2009
Darth Naga posts what may be the first online video chilli review at ChileFoundry.co.uk.

2004
thehotpepper.com internet forum launches.

1994
The first super-hot chilli is officially named when the Red Savina chilli is confirmed as the hottest chilli in the world by the Guinness World Records with a Scoville rating of 500,000 SHU.

1492
Christopher Columbus discovers chillies in the Caribbean.

1500s
Physician to King Felipe II of Spain brings chilli plants to Spain from the New World. Spanish and Portuguese traders sell them to North Africa, West Africa, India and the Far East.

1600s
Chillies reach every part of the globe.

Early 1800s
First bottled chilli sauce sold in America.

1868
In Louisiana, Edmund McIlhenny combines aged red peppers, Avery Island salt and distilled vinegar to create Tabasco sauce.

1898
Pure capsaicin extracted for the first time by scientist Karl Micko.

1976
International Chili Society formed with headquarters in Newport Beach, California.

1980
David Tran establishes Huy Fong Foods in LA and creates Sriracha Hot Chili Sauce.

1988
Le Saucier, the first shop dedicated to chilli sauces is opened by Lisa Lamme in Faneuil Hall Marketplace in Boston, Massachusetts.

1988
First National Fiery Foods Show held in El Paso, Texas.

1992
Chile Pepper Institute created on the campus of the New Mexico State University to carry out education and research related to capsicums.

1992
Capsaicin extract is added to hot sauce for the first time by Dave Hirschkop to make Dave's Insanity Sauce.

1989
Jersey Shore bartender Blair Lazar creates ultra-hot Blair's Death Sauce.

SOME LIKE IT HOT
DECODING THE SCOVILLE SCALE

Chilli is unique in the fruit world for having its very own system of measurement. How cool is that? The Scoville Scale was invented in 1912 by American chemist Wilbur Scoville specifically to measure a chilli's spicy heat (or 'pungency', as the men in white coats call it).

Although dear Wilbur was a top-flight scientist with some serious credentials, the Scoville scale is based on what now looks like pretty shaky methodology. Basically, the Scoville organoleptic test involves taking a precise amount of dried chilli that's been dissolved in alcohol to extract the heat-giving capsaicin chemical compound, diluting it in sugar-water. The chilli that needs the most amount of water before your chums can no longer taste it is the winner.

The degree of dilution is then measured in Scoville units (SHU). So, a red pepper that you'd slice up for your salad rates zero on the scale because it contains no capsaicin so doesn't have to be diluted at all, but a Bhut Jolokia has to be diluted a million times – that's about 50 litres (88 pints) of water to one drop of the dissolved chilli – before it's undetectable. Therefore it gets a rating of 1,000,000 SHU.

This may all sound very scientific, but there's a problem. Everyone's sense of taste is slightly different, plus you can build up a resistance to the effects of capsaicin over the course of a tasting session. So even though this method uses a panel of five trained tasters, results can differ by as much as 50 per cent from lab to lab.

If you're thinking, 'It's a hundred years later, couldn't we come up with something better?' then you're right. High Performance Liquid Chromatography (HPLC) cuts out human error and replaces it with boxes, switches, tubes and reinforced steel columns. By pumping a liquid sample of the chilli through a specially lined steel column, scientists can measure exactly the amount of capsaicin present, which is expressed in American Spice Trade Association (ASTA) Pungency Units. Nevertheless, everyone still uses Wilbur's scale, so the ASTA units are multiplied by 15 to get the Scoville equivalent.

CAROLINA REAPER: 2,200,000 SHU

MORUGA SCORPION: 2,009,231

TRINIDAD SCORPION: 1,463,700

BHUT JOLOKIA: 1,041,427

HABAÑERO: 200,000-385,000

SCOTCH BONNET: 150,000-325,000

BIRD'S EYE: 100,000-225,000

THAI: 50,000-100,000

CAYENNE: 30,000-50,000

DE-ÁRBOL: 15,000-30,000

CHIPOTLE: 5,000-8,000

JALAPEÑO: 2,500-8,000

PEPERONCINI: 100-500

BELL PEPPER: 0 SHU

THE 10 HOTTEST CHILLIES IN THE WORLD

1 CAROLINA REAPER
2,200,000 SHU
Enjoy the sweet fruity flavour of this unholy cross between a Pakistani Naga and a Red Habañero before it sets your mouth alight. Developed by the all too accurately named Pucker Butt Pepper Company of South Carolina, this scorpion-tailed bumpy-red-skinned devil was certified hottest chilli by the Guinness Book of World Records in 2013.

2 MORUGA SCORPION
2,009,231 SHU
The chilli formerly known as the hottest on the planet doesn't come from the depths of hell but from the south central coast of Trinidad. Growing to the size of a golf ball, like the Carolina Reaper this pepper comes on like a fruit but hides a great big hot sting in its tail.

3 7 POT BRAIN STRAIN
1,900,000 SHU
Named after its supposed resemblance to a human brain (you should worry if that's what's actually inside your head), this round, bumpy-skinned beast packs serious heat. In Trinidad, they call it '7 pot' because one chilli is enough to flavour seven pots of stew.

4 7 POT PRIMO
1,900,000 SHU
This cross breed of the Naga Morich from India and the Trinidad 7 Pot has been cultivated by Southern rocker Troy 'Primo' Primeaux of cult band Santeria in Louisiana since 2005. Sure, there's floral notes, but the finish is as hot as one of Primo's ear-shredding guitar licks.

5 POD DOUGLAH
1,853,936 SHU
This rare chocolate brown strain is often cited as one of the best tasting of the super-hot chillies, that is until it takes your sense of taste away with the ferocious heat that's contained within the copious interior membrane.

6 TRINIDAD SCORPION BUTCH T
1,463,700 SHU
This variant on the Trinidad Scorpion is named after Zydeco farms and hot sauce company owner Butch Taylor who propagates the seeds in Crosby, Mississippi. A one-time Guinness record holder, Butch Ts are so hot that it's said the cooks making sauce with the fiery blighters are forced to wear protective body suits.

7 NAGA VIPER
1,349,000 SHU
This shiny red firecracker isn't grown in hot climes, but in Cumbria in the north of England. Gerald Fowler of The Chilli Pepper Company crossed Naga Morich, Bhut Jolokia and Trinidad Scorpion to create this bitingly hot strain.

8 BHUT JOLOKIA (GHOST PEPPER)
1,041,427 SHU
The Justin Bieber of the chilli world, the media frenzy surrounding the Bhut Jolokia when it first burst onto the scene in 2007 means that many still believe its the hottest in the world. Maybe it's not, but maybe it'll still blow your head clean off.

9. 7 POD BARRACKPORE
1,000,070 SHU
Originating from Barrackpore in Trinidad, this is closely related to the Moruga Scorpion but has a more elongated pod shape. While not quite reaching the dizzying heights of the insane heat of some other chillies on this list, still approach this one with caution.

RED SAVINA HABAÑERO
500,000 SHU
Back in the day, Red Savina, out of Walnut, California, was the world champion chilli, holding the hottest title from 1994 until it was beaten by the Jolokia in 2007. It might not be breaking records any more, but it still has knock-out flavour and punchy heat.

CHILLI HEAD SCIENCE

Eating chillies provokes a physical response like no other foodstuff. I mean, when was the last time you cried when you ate a banana (and no, I don't mean when you were snacking while watching *Marley and Me*)? We're all familiar with the burn, the perspiration and the runny nose, but how on earth can such a tiny fruit have such a big impact? Science has the answer.

It's all down to a chemical called capsaicin that's found only in chillies and mainly in the pepper's placental tissue, the membrane that holds the seeds. Discovered in 1816, this colourless, odourless compound also goes by the catchy name of (E)-N-(4-Hydroxy-3-methoxybenzyl)-8-methylnon-6-enamide. Probably best stick with capsaicin then. It's made up of seven different chemical components which produce the different sensations, picked up not by taste buds but by pain receptors in the mouth, including the bite at the back of the palate and throat and the slow burn on the tongue.

Capsaicin is a chemical irritant that causes a burning sensation in any tissue it comes in contact with, including your mucus membrane, hence the runny nose and your lacrimal (tear) gland, and hence the weeping. It also triggers heat-related pain receptors

in the body which send signals via the spinal cord to the brain which responds by trying to cool the body down, so you begin to flush and sweat.

One thing you really need to know about capsaicin is that it's hydrophobic. Imagine for some reason, perhaps because you're certifiable, you've eaten a curry made with Carolina Reapers, the world's hottest chilli. The burn has spread from your tongue to the roof of your mouth, your teeth feel like they're going to fall out and the fire is making its way down your throat towards your stomach. You grab a bottle of water and down it in one. To your horror, it has no effect, in fact you feel worse. That's because capsaicin won't dissolve in water. But it does dissolve in fats or oils, so far better to have some full cream milk at the ready, or a glass of lassi, the Indian yoghurt drink. If you can stand the idea, a spoonful or two of olive oil is also extremely effective.

Although all this points to a deep stream of masochism among Chilli Heads, there are some more obvious chemically related pleasures to eating chillies. To defend itself against all that capsaicin-related pain, the body releases endorphins, naturally produced painkillers that can result in a light-headed euphoric high, especially after digesting a super-hot chilli. The endorphin reaction also means the humble chilli is of increasing interest to the medical profession, where capsaicin is being used to help treat everything from arthritis to psoriasis.

CHILLI QUOTES

'People with chilli peppers on their chef pants shouldn't be allowed in the kitchen.'

Chef April Bloomfield

'I like chilli, but not enough to discuss it with someone from Texas.'

Food writer Calvin Trillin

'Next to music there is nothing that lifts the spirits and strengthens the soul more than a good bowl of chilli.'

Harry James (1916–1983), band leader and trumpeter

'I'm so high but I feel so crappy.'

Online chilli reviewer Ted Barrus describing the endorphin rush from eating two of Ed Currie's Death Strain chillies

'Wish I had time for just one more bowl of chilli.'

Dying words of frontiersman Kit Carson (1809–1868)

'We may come to enjoy our body's negative responses to situations when we realise that there is no, or minimal, actual danger. In the case of the roller coaster, our body is scared, and sympathetically activated, but we know we are safe. Similarly for our crying in sad movies, and the burn we feel with chilli pepper.'

Paul Rozin, Professor of Psychology, University of Pennsylvania

'Chilli is much improved by having had a day to contemplate its fate.'

Author John Steele Gordon

'Chilli represents your three stages of matter: solid, liquid and eventually gas.'

Actor John Goodman as Dan Conner in the 90s TV series Roseanne

'The aroma of good chilli should generate rapture akin to a lover's kiss.'

Motto of the Chili Appreciation Society International

'Most people think about chillies in terms of their heat and their capacity to blow one's head off. I think about how they can delicately pep up a pile of silky aubergines.'

Thomasina Miers, cook and founder of Wahaca

CHILLI BEEF RAMEN

In recent years, the Japanese noodle soup ramen has been popularised by Korean American chef David Chang at his international Momofuku restaurant group and in the UK by the Wagamama chain. The real thing is a labour of love, involving making spiced stock, tare (a type of teriyaki sauce), dashi (seaweed and dried tuna stock) roast pork belly and even your own noodles all from scratch. The following is a much simplified version but delicious nonetheless, and replacing the slow-cooked pork with quickly seared steak makes the dish easier and faster to prepare. Committed Chilli Heads can make their own version of Hell Ramen, a type of ultra-hot noodle soup served in some ramen shops in Japan by increasing the amount and type of chilli sauce to taste.

INGREDIENTS

- 8 spring onions, finely sliced
- 150g (5oz) store-bought Japanese steamed fish cake, sliced
- 225g (8oz) can bamboo shoots, drained
- 100g (4oz) baby spinach, washed and drained
- 4 eggs, poached
- 2 x 200g (8oz) sirloin steaks
- 1 tbsp sunflower oil
- Ultimate Chilli Head Sauce (see page 66) or chilli or teriyaki sauce of your choice
- 600g (1lb 5oz) fresh ramen or 500g (1lb 2oz) dried egg noodles
- 2 litres (4 pints) fresh chicken stock
- Sliced fresh chilli of your choice, to garnish

1 Prepare the spring onions, fish cake, bamboo shoots, spinach and poached eggs.

2 Heat a large frying pan until screaming hot (you should see smoke rising from it). Season the steaks. Add the sunflower oil to the pan and fry the steaks for 2–3 minutes on each side for medium rare or to your liking. Remove to a warmed plate, and brush both sides with the chilli sauce. Cover loosely with tin foil and leave to rest for 5 minutes.

3 Cook the ramen or dried egg noodles as per the packet instructions and drain. Bring the chicken stock to the boil. Place 1 tsp of the chilli sauce into each of 4 large bowls. Pour over 500ml (17fl oz) of the hot stock and whisk to amalgamate the sauce. Add a quarter of the spinach and noodles to each bowl. Divide the beef between the bowls, laying it in neat overlapping slices on top of the noodles. Top each bowl with a poached egg, 2 slices of fish cake, a quarter of the spring onions and a few slices of fresh chilli. Serve with more chilli sauce on the side.

PIRI PIRI CHICKEN

Made world famous by the Portuguese-inspired Nando's restaurant chain, this spicy dish gets its name from the sauce that's made with fiery African Bird's Eye chillies that are also known as Piri Piri chillies, the spelling used for the dish in Africa. They are essential to the dish and available online from sites including Hot Stuff Chilli Company (www.hotstuffchillicompany.co.uk). If you want more heat, add additional African Bird's Eyes or change it up with Scotch Bonnet or Dorset Naga.

SERVES 4

INGREDIENTS

- 1 red onion, roughly chopped
- 2 large tomatoes, peeled and de-seeded
- 2 African Bird's Eye chillies
- 3 garlic cloves, peeled
- 1 tbsp sweet smoked paprika
- 100ml (3½fl oz) olive oil
- Juice of 1–2 lemons
- 1 tsp thyme leaves
- 1 whole medium chicken (or 8 chicken thighs)
- Salt and sugar

1 First make the piri piri sauce. Place the onion, tomatoes, chillies, garlic, paprika, olive oil, lemon juice and thyme leaves in a blender. Blend until smooth, then add salt and sugar to taste. Transfer to a pan, bring to the boil, simmer for 10 minutes and then allow to cool.

2 Spatchcock the chicken: cut out the backbone with poultry scissors and press down on the breast bone to flatten. Slash across the legs (or thighs, if using) with a sharp knife several times nearly down to the bone. Place in a baking dish and pour over the sauce. Rub in all over the chicken. Leave to marinate for 1 hour; ideally overnight.

3 Roast in the oven at 180°C/350°F/Gas mark 4 for 1 hour or until tender. Serve with chips and a green salad, with any leftover sauce spooned over.

Note If you want extra piri piri sauce to use as a condiment, double the quantities, then divide into two. Use one batch to marinate the chicken and the other as a condiment.

CHILLI TRIVIA

Cosmonaut Yuri I. Malenchenko and astronaut Edward T. Lu were probably the first Chilli Heads in space. A photograph on Nasa's website (tinyurl.com/qc9jkd7) of a meal they shared aboard the International Space Station in 2003 shows a bottle of Sriracha sauce floating in the background.

Legend has it that the outlaw Jesse James refused to rob a bank in McKinney, Texas because the town was home to his favourite chilli parlour.

Avoid cold feet on a skiing trip by lining your socks with cayenne. The pepper causes blood vessels in your feet to dilate, improving blood flow and so making your toes toasty.

African farmers prevent elephants damaging their crops by burning briquettes of animal dung and crushed chillies. The pachyderms won't come near the farms because they are allergic to the capsaicin in the chillies.

The most famous chilli con carne in the world was made at the now closed Chasen's restaurant in Hollywood. It's claimed that Elizabeth Taylor was such a big fan, she had several gallons of the stuff shipped at great expense to Rome in the early 1960s where she was filming the movie Cleopatra.

CHILLI IS THE SECOND MOST USED CONDIMENT IN THE WORLD, SECOND ONLY TO SALT.

Texans love chillies so much that the state has two official peppers. Jalapeño was designated Official Pepper of Texas in 1995 while the wild-growing, tiny Chiltepin was named Official Native Pepper of Texas in 1997.

According to the scientific journal *Toxicon*, if you weigh 63kg (9st 9lb) or less and drink 1.5 litres (2½ pints) of Louisiana-style hot sauce you will die of respiratory failure.

Five showjumpers were disqualified from the 2008 Olympics for rubbing their horses with a cream containing capsaicin. The chemical makes the horse's legs hypersensitive so they jump higher to avoid the pain of hitting the barriers.

Birds are the only creatures not sensitive to capsaicin.

That means they're happy to keep pecking at chillies and spilling the seeds and eating them, helping to propagate the plants as they poop them out wherever they go.

In 2009, the Guardian newspaper reported that police in China were handing out chillies to drivers at service stations to help them stay awake on the roads. The move was inspired by Chairman Mao, who ate chillies at night to keep him alert while he was writing his famous little red book.

CHILLIES FOR SALE

THE MUST-HAVE CHILLI STUFF

Manufacturers and producers haven't been slow to pick up on the Chilli Head cult. You could fill your house with what there is out there. From high fashion to trash, from the useful to the useless, it's all available to buy. Credit cards at the ready Chilli Heads: one two, three... BUY!

ABSINTHE RED CHILLI HEAD

Want to get completely off your rocker while simultaneously enjoying a capsaicin kick? Then look no further than this luridly red and highly alcoholic (a whopping 55 per cent proof) liquor that comes in a wicked skull-shaped bottle, complete with floating red chilli. Available from absinthes.com.

ROCK OUT SHOES

Be the height of fashion while proclaiming your love for the world's trendiest hot sauce in these high quality Sriracha-themed high heels. The red, white and green colour scheme mimics the famous bottle, with the lettering and rooster logo cleverly integrated into the shoe's design. Available from hourglassfootwear.com.

CHILLI WILLY

At some point, haven't we all thought, 'why oh why isn't there a chilli that looks frighteningly like a horribly sunburnt male member?' Well, you're in luck! Presenting Chilli Willy, the naturally growing chilli that's about ten times hotter than a Jalapeño and available as seeds or in kit form. Sadly, this cock-shaped capsicum has arrived 20 years too late to appear on the unusually shaped vegetable spot on *That's Life!* (ask your mother). Available from chilli-willy.com.

CHILLI BEER

Almost too obvious an idea, there are numerous chilli beers brewed around the world. One of the fastest-growing UK brands is Fallen Angel from Sussex. Far from being novelty brews, Black Death stout with Naga, Fire in the Hole ale with fresh hot green chillies and Scotch Bonnet cider are all well made and delicious. Available from fallenangelbrewery.com.

AD-HOC CHILLI MILL

The design of this acrylic mill is eye-catching for all the wrong reasons. Standing erect on a metallic base and with a long, tapering top, you might think this gadget that dispenses dried chillies had been designed for an entirely different sort of grinding. Available from lakeland.co.uk and not Ann Summers.

CHILLI BOTTLE STOPPER

As unlikely as it seems, some people don't finish a bottle of wine after they've opened it (it's true! Just track down a sensible person and ask them) so what could be better to prevent your Chateau Petrus 1961 from going off in the fridge overnight than a red chilli-shaped bottle stopper. The perfect Christmas gift for, well, someone. Available from chilligifts.co.uk.

CHILLI THOM ARTWORK

Chilli Thom is an artist based in Whistler, Canada whose dreamy psychedelic landscapes are inspired by British Columbia's incredible wildness. Although he doesn't paint chillies as such, his work and especially his trees are littered with chilli shapes. Available from chilithom.com.

CHILLI-SHAPED SALSA BOWL

Proudly serve your finest homemade salsa to your Chilli Head friends in a lidded bowl that looks just like a chilli. It's a genuine hoot. Available from Amazon.

CHILLI PARTY GAMES

Get your Chilli Head party off to a swing by bashing this papier-mâché red chilli shaped pinata to bits. (Available from amazon. com). Fill with red hot chilli-shaped jellies from firebox.com, who also stock the fun Instant Regret Chocolate Roulette game where you take turns choosing a milk chocolate bullet, only one of which is charged with a 1 million SHU chilli extract.

TABASCO CHOCOLATE

Made by McIlhenny Co themselves, these chunky wedges of spicy chocolate come in an attractive branded circular tin. From Amazon.

CHILLI ALCHEMIST SAUCES

This range of seven sauces, created by Clifton Chilli Club member Jay Webley, stands out from the crowd with its hand-corked, wax-sealed apothecary bottles. With flavours including Anise (beetroot, fennel, red wine and red Habañero chillies) and Elixir Orientem (lemongrass, ginger and Thai red chillies), they taste good too. Available from chillialchemist.co.uk.

MAKE YOUR OWN ORGANIC CHILLI GINGER BEER

A do-it-yourself kit with everything you need to brew your own deliciously hot ginger beer. Available from notonthehighstreet.com.

CHILLI MAGNET PENS

A pair of ballpoint pens shaped like long chillies, one red, one green and both magnetic so they'll stick around long after your girlfriend leaves you because she's sick of all the chilli-themed junk you keep on buying. Available from Amazon.

RING OF FIRE AFTER-CURRY WIPES

Just what you need after a night on the phall. These are basically the same wet wipes you'd use to wipe a baby's bum but bigger. Well, they'd need to be, wouldn't they? Available from menkind.co.uk.

JOINING THE CLAN

CHILLI HEAD INITIATION
SEVEN STEPS TO CHILLI HEAD HEAVEN

Everyone loves a little bit of chilli now and then, but Chilli Heads are a breed apart. They eat, sleep and think chillies 24/7. If you want to join this obsessive sect there are a few easy things you need to do to get yourself accepted. You've already taken the first step by buying this book, and by the time you finish it you'll be ready to hold your head up high in the hottest and more esteemed Chilli Head company. Follow these seven easy steps to Chilli Head heaven.

STEP 1
FOLLOW YOUR FELLOW CHILLI HEADS

@puckerbutt Smokin' Ed Currie, founder of the PuckerButt Pepper Company in Fort Mill, South Carolina, developed Smokin Ed's Carolina Reaper, currently the hottest chilli in the world.

@chilliheat Gerald Fowler, owner of the Chilli Pepper Company in Cumbria, UK supplying sauces and seeds including his own Naga Viper, currently the seventh hottest chilli in the world.

@Pepperboy143 Vic Clinco, owner of what is probably the largest collection of chilli sauces in the world (6,000 bottles and counting) and a regular contributor to Chile Pepper magazine.

@scottroberts Chilli Head extraordinaire. Posts hot sauce, spicy food and BBQ reviews at scottrobertsweb.com and hosts the Firecast podcast at weeklyfirecast.com.

@fieryworldken Ken Alexander, leading blogger. Read his posts at It's a Fiery World (fieryworld.com).

@HomeGrownUkChil Leo Scott. Fearless British hot sauce video reviewer.

@Tedbarrus Also known as The Fire Breathing Idiot. Top American sauce and 'pod' (fresh chilli) reviewer.

STEP 2 BOOKMARK THESE WEBSITES

Fiery Foods and Barbecue Supersite (fiery-foods.com) Home of Chilli Head legend, author, Fiery Foods show and Scovie Awards founder Dave DeWitt (@FieryFoods) and his podcasts.

The Chile Foundry (chilefoundry.com) Leading UK-based chilli website with articles, product reviews and A-Z guides to chilli businesses around the world.

Eat More Heat (eatmoreheat.com) Founded by 'Leader of the heatards' James Wreck (@JamesWreck) for his 'in-depth reviews of spicy hot food, sauces, peppers, restaurants or anything else that makes your mouth burn'.

Peppers.com The number one internet resource for chilli sauces.

Thechileman.org The home of the world's most comprehensive, fully illustrated chilli database.

START YOUR CHILLI HEAD LIBRARY

A Bowl of Red **by Frank X Tolbert** A history of chilli con carne written by the late Frank X Tolbert, a Dallas-based newspaper columnist who founded the World Chilli Championship in 1967.

The Chile Pepper Encyclopedia **by Dave DeWitt** Written by America's leading chilli expert, this book covers all the expected bases as well as including 100 recipes.

The Hot Book of Chillies **by David Floyd** Written by the founder of chilefoundry.com, this book covers the history of chilli and lists about 100 of the most popular varieties.

Growing Chillies **by Jason Nickles** Everything you need to know about growing chillies at home.

Hot Sauce **by Jennifer Trainer Thompson** Techniques and recipes for making your own signature hot sauces.

SUBSCRIBE TO CHILE PEPPER MAGAZINE

Covers recipes and products with articles on how to grow your own chillies. Published in the USA, the magazine ships internationally and is available as an app and digital download. Subscribe at chilepepper. com.

JOIN THE THEHOTPEPPER.COM

With nearly ten thousand members worldwide, this very active forum is the place to come and discuss your chilli obsession online. Discussions cover every aspect of Chilli Head-ism from cooking to growing, product reviews to events.

STEP 6

BECOME A MEMBER OF A CHILLI CLUB

Either the International Chili Society (chilicookoff.com) or the British Chilli Growing Society (britishchilligrowingsociety.org).

 STEP 7

DON THE GARB OF THE CHILLI HEAD

Check out websites including highseastrading.com, cafepress.com and packershoes.com and deck yourself out head to toe in chilli-themed clothing from bandanas to boxer shorts, from Hawaiian shirts to chilli pepper Reeboks.

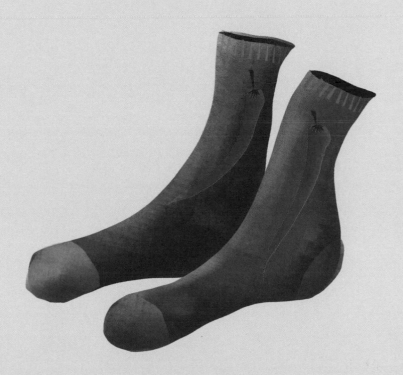

WORLD'S BEST CHILLI FESTS

Globally, chilli festivals are growing in number and popularity year on year, and a visit to at least one is a crucial part of the Chilli Head experience. Not only will you get to meet your fellow chilli obsessives but you'll be sure to bump into some of the big names on the scene including growers, sauce makers and reviewers. These festivals are the best place to try numerous chilli products all in one place, and often there's a chance to watch or even take part in a chilli eating competition.

UK

You could spend August and early September hopping from one chilli fest to the next. Highlights of the season include the two-day Upton Cheyney Chilli and Cider Festival, Bristol (uptonchilli.co.uk) which includes the Clifton Chilli Club's chilli-eating competition and

the UK Chilli Cook-Off Association competition, the premiere chilli con carne cooking competition in the UK.

Also not to be missed is the West Dean Chilli Fiesta in West Sussex (westdean.org.uk). In 2014, a record 12,000 people attended the event on just one day of the three-day festival. Set in the rolling Sussex countryside in the grounds of West Dean College, this is an idyllic setting for demos, live music, some great spicy food and the chance to tour the College's gardens where they grow hundreds of varieties of chillies.

For a more urban experience, head to Festival of Heat in Spitalfields City Farm, London (thefestivalofheat.co.uk) where the line-up includes chilli demos, debates and workshops as well as live folk music, a picnic area and plenty to entertain the kids.

ITALY

For five whole days in September, the coastal town of Diamante in Calabria, Southern Italy becomes a mecca for Chilli Heads when it stages the Peperoncino Festival (peperoncinofestival.org). This is not just a celebration of the locally grown, mildly hot peperoncino chilli, but a full-on orgy of spice with chillies of all varieties, eating competitions, a spicy film festival and chilli-based satire, whatever that is. You could even win a prize for your chilli thesis.

FINLAND

The growing appetite for hot foods in Finland is being fed by Chilifest Finland (chilifest.fi). Staged in Tampere in the south of the country in August by Finnish chilli importer Oy Poppamies, the free festival includes all the expected vendors with their sauces and seeds plus the Naga Morich Eating World Championship and the Chillirock open air concert.

USA

In America, you have to visit what is probably the most atmospheric setting for not one but two of the most prestigious chilli cook-offs in the world. Terlingua is a genuine ghost town, an abandoned mining community in the Texas desert close to the Mexican border. In the first week of November, it plays host to the Chili Appreciation Society International's Chili Championship (chili.org) and the Original Terlingua Frank X. Tolbert–Wick Fowler Championship Chili Cookoff (abowlofred.com), both established for more than four decades. There's a real party atmosphere, so wear your best fancy dress costume if you want to fit in.

Held over two days in March or April in central Manhattan, the New York Hot Sauce Expo (nychotsauceexpo.com) features dozens

of vendors, numerous chilli challenges and the Screaming Mi Mi Hot Sauce Awards. Hatch in New Mexico calls itself the 'Chile Capital of the World' and its crop of green chillies is highly prized by chilli connoisseurs. The Hatch Valley Chile Festival (hatchchilefest. com) in late August attracts Chilli Heads from all over the world and the line-up includes contests, cook-offs, live entertainment and a Saturday night dance.

AUSTRALIA

With culinary influences from chilli-loving South East Asia, Australia has its fair share of chilli festivals. The annual two-day LiveLighter Araluen's Fremantle Chilli Festival (araluenbotanicpark.com.au) held on the Esplanade in Fremantle near Perth claims to be the country's largest and most successful chilli festival with nearly 100 stall holders, cooking demonstrations from local chefs and live entertainment. Established for more than 15 years, the Saw Tell Chilli Festival (sawtellchillifestival.com.au) is held in July in the beautiful coastal village of Saw Tell in New South Wales where the main street is lined with stallholders selling everything from chilli ginger beer to chilli chocolate balls.

IN THE CLUB
HOW TO FORM YOUR OWN CHILLI HEAD SOCIETY

There's nothing Chilli Heads like better than hanging out with other Chilli Heads, exchanging rumours about the latest super-hot F1s, gossiping about who can't take the heat and planning the next chilli-related trip over a beer or two. But there's much more to forming your own Chilli Head Society than just hanging out with your mates in the pub. Actually, thinking about it, there isn't much more to it, so what are you waiting for? Mine's a pint of craft lager by the way.

But what starts off as a sociable night on the lash can turn into something altogether more exciting, as the Bristol, UK-based Clifton Chilli Club have proved. And we're not talking about the time they went to that 'gentleman's club' after last orders. Jay 'Chilli Head' Webley joined the club soon after it was launched back in summer 2009 by founding members Jim Booth, Dave MacDonald and the man known only as 'Chilli Dave'.

'They all lived within a few roads of each other at the time and used to drink in a local pub,' explains Webley, who also runs the Chilli Alchemist sauce company. They heard about an open day at the Sea Spring Seeds chilli farm in Dorset, enjoyed their visit and decided to form a club. 'I'd had a passion for chillies for a few years and joined and since then more and more of us have become involved,' continues Webley.

'There's about eight core members that are actively working for and promoting the club but as far as people who call themselves members it's a tricky thing to put a number on. Our Facebook page has over 10,000 likes and currently we have an open membership

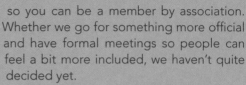

so you can be a member by association. Whether we go for something more official and have formal meetings so people can feel a bit more included, we haven't quite decided yet.

'We don't limit our activities to Clifton and Bristol,' says Webley, 'we've got friends all over the country. So when we're out and about doing festivals, there are a lot of local volunteers who will come along and help out as honorary members.

'We run the club on an informal basis but everyone plays their part. Chilli Dave has a military background and he takes care of the formal structured side of things, I'm more involved in the social media side of things, Dave Mac helps a lot with treasury and logistics – travel arrangements and so forth – and Jim is the front man when we're at festivals and compering.'

All the core members grow chillies at home and in addition maintain a polytunnel on an allotment and a polytunnel at the Upton Cheyney Chilli Farm near Bristol where they also help out on a voluntary basis.

'The growth of the club has been quite organic. As a club we would go to festivals as punters and get to chat with the producers and network and that led to one of our first gigs – the chilli eating competition at the Grillstock festival in Bristol. Chilli Fest UK saw what we did at Grillstock, liked it and wanted to integrate the competition with the festivals they run all over the country. We're quite a well oiled machine when it comes to the competitions because we can do everything from sourcing the peppers to promoting the festival through social media to actually running the event.'

The club's profile has been raised with appearances on a Radio 4 documentary and celebrity baker Paul Hollywood's TV series. The club is also expanding operations internationally with a filmed report from the Peperoncino Festival in Diamante, Calabria, Italy and plans to visit the Houston Hot Sauce festival and have their own live video show from the Hot Sauce Expo in New York.

You may not want to go to quite the lengths of the Clifton Chilli Club, but let their meteoric rise and impressive raft of activities be an inspiration to you and your mates to get out of the pub and make your own club a reality. But in the meantime, another pint . . . ?

HOW TO BECOME A CHILLI-EATING CHAMPION

Want to make a name for yourself with a world record for eating chillies? Then you're going to have to go some. In 2013 Jason McNabb, a dentist from Louisville, was invited to appear on the World's Records Unleashed TV programme in a ghost pepper-eating contest. Even though one of his two competitors was professional competitive eater Kevin Ross (known for ludicrous challenges like downing a gallon of milk while performing physical jerks), McNabb prevailed, munching through 66g (2.3oz) (between 12 and 15 chillies; apparently no one thought to count) of the searingly hot pepper in the two-minute time limit.

In an interview with a local paper, McNabb revealed that he'd trained for the event by eating as many ghost peppers as he could in a minute, but made the mistake of doing so once on an empty stomach, resulting in his face turning white, severe stomach cramps and profuse sweating.

'Some people think drinking milk will help but actually you need some carbohydrate like a banana in your stomach,' says Ed Currie, creator of the Carolina Reaper, who eats 8–12 super-hot chillies a day. 'That, along with your stomach acid and saliva, will break up the capsaicin and you'll avoid the cramps. As far as your mouth goes, there's nothing you can do to keep from burning, but after you've eaten a chilli you can drink some lemon or lime juice and that will help break up the oils stuck on your tongue and in your mouth and that makes it go away a little faster.'

Currie is not a competitive eater himself as he describes himself as 'broken', meaning that his unnaturally high tolerance to capsaicin would give him an unfair advantage (he claims to have eaten seven Carolina Reapers in 25 seconds). 'You definitely build up a tolerance,' he explains. 'It's like being a boxer, if you get hit all day long every day, after a while it doesn't bother you. It still hurts but you've got to keep on doing your job. But you can lose that tolerance too. A friend of mine had mouth ulcers and had to stop eating chillies for a while and then couldn't eat super-hots.'

But Jay Webley, who helps organise the Chilli Fest UK chilli-eating competitions, reckons there's an argument for not being prepared at all. 'We've found that the secret to winning is to be female and to have never competed before.'

The theory is partly borne out by Paula Turzanski, the first woman to win the Club's Clash of the Titans competition which she did in 2013, beating nine other international competitors. Although it was her first competition, she told a local paper that she was a keen eater of chillies and had been building her tolerance for years. The key to her win, she said, was to sample a bit of all the chillies ahead of competing.

With chilli-eating competitions being staged all over the world, including the Nagaland Chilli Eating Competition in India where, in 2014, Chetie Khiamnungyan won 25,000 rupees by eating 18.5 Naga chillies, there's no excuse for a truly committed Chilli Head not to give it a go. Just don't enter on an empty stomach.

YOUCHILLI
HOW TO SET UP YOUR OWN CHILLI REVIEW CHANNEL

Love chillies and chilli sauce? Never want to pay to eat them again? Then set up your own chilli review channel. With a minimum of equipment and know-how, you could be transmitting your opinions of free samples of the latest chilli products worldwide within days. YouTube chilli stars like Ted 'The Fire Breathing Idiot' Barrus have accumulated tens of thousands of subscribers and hundreds of thousands of views for their short videos. With those sorts of figures, you could even earn money from your efforts.

Tony Ainsworth, a tech support analyst, is better known to Chilli Heads around the world as Darth Naga (Tony is a Star Wars geek and his favourite chilli is, well you can guess), one of the UK's leading spicy reviewers. His career began in 2008 after visiting the West Dean Chilli Fiesta for the first time and tasted Hot-Headz sauces. Inspired, he set up a Facebook appreciation page which came to the attention of David Floyd, editor of the chilefoundry.com online magazine.

'He asked me to write a review of a product, he liked it and took me on as a staff writer. One day we got a sample in of pure Naga Jolokia paste. It was so hot I suggested we do a video review. I already had a camera and there weren't many people doing them at the time so David agreed. We realised that people loved seeing me in pain and we went from there.'

Tony is self-taught and makes his videos at home using a £500 camcorder with an inbuilt microphone. He films in natural light so there's no need for expensive additional lighting equipment. The only other kit he uses is a tripod and an inexpensive video-editing software package. Setting up your own YouTube channel is free and Tony has built on his Chile Foundry following via Twitter and Facebook. Having made contacts through the internet and visiting festivals, he gets sent nearly everything he reviews for free.

The review format is simple: introduce the product and, if it's a sauce, pour a decent amount onto a spoon (Chilli Heads don't want to see their reviewers wimp out), eat and then try and describe the aroma, flavour and heat before you start writhing on the floor in pain. A good tip is to get the review done in one take, as Tony explains.

'When I reviewed the Naga purée, which was about 1 million SHU, I ate a heaped teaspoon and went through agony. I watched it back and realised I wasn't looking at the camera but at the monitor screen to the side. I forced myself to do it again and half an hour later stomach cramps began to kick in. I stumbled down to the toilet and next thing I knew I woke up naked in the foetal position with my clothes folded neatly beside me and with the door locked. I think I'd gone endorphin mad and blacked out.'

There are other more prosaic risks to testing super-hot sauces and whole chillies (in his time, Tony has eaten a whole Carolina Reaper and Naga Viper on screen). 'I used to let stuff go through my system and deal with the obvious fall-out the other end. But I've had such extreme products, especially ones with super-hot capsaicin extract in them, that they've irritated my bowels so much I've passed blood. So after the review I bring them back up.'

Although Tony keeps that particular process off camera, many reviews include 'vomit warnings' and are all the more popular for them. 'I've always got a bucket handy for stupidly hot stuff that my body rejects while I'm filming. I used to edit it out but I got so many messages from people saying "we want to see you throw up" that now I video my "vom reactions". It's the same thing as laughing at someone when they fall off their bike – it's weird but I think we gain comfort sometimes from seeing other people in pain.'

Tony's Darth Naga reviews have not only helped him build a chilli sauce collection but have led to work at chilli festivals around the UK, compering chilli-eating competitions and he's appeared on a TV series about spicy food with comedian Omid Djalili. 'I've got a full-time job so I haven't felt the inclination to make YouTube my career yet. My hobby is doing the videos, purely for the love of it. Although I'm not getting paid, I never run out of the product that I love.'

THE MOST EXTREME CHILLI-EATING VIDEOS ON THE NET

 ## CHILE BEAST: I EAT 40+ DRIED CAROLINA REAPERS. NEW WORLD RECORD EXTREMELY PAINFUL!!!!

The Chile Beast specialises in extreme challenges and frankly needs to be saved from himself. Any one of his uploads is painful to watch, but the extreme sweat, free-flowing mucus and psychotic stares to camera are gruesome to behold. This video is topped only by his Dried Carolina Reaper Aftermath Extreme Vomit Alert (youtube.com/watch?v=CP0kTVqwjxA) which gives Mr Creosote in *Monty Python's The Meaning of Life* a run for his money.

youtube.com/watch?v=DyGuh6WEvPQ

DAN DARES DRINKS A GLASS OF DAVE'S INSANITY GHOST PEPPER CHILLI SAUCE WARNING EXTREME

British spice daredevil Dan describes the effects of half a tumbler full of Dave's Insanity in an increasingly tremulous voice as the full horror of his action dawns on him. 'You could really cook an egg in my mouth right now, that's how hot my tongue feels.' Dan at least has the good manners to duck out of view while he deals with the after effects.

youtube.com/watch?v=TWA-hQvoOGE0

EATING THE HOTTEST PEPPER IN THE WORLD, THE BHUT JOLOKIA

Jamie Kocher, CEO of the Waimea Bay Chili Pepper Company, eats the 'intestinal tract' of a Bhut Jolokia. First he's hopping mad, then he's trying to meditate through the pain, then he's on the couch in the foetal position. An hour later he's asking to be taken to the hospital. Harrowing.

youtube.com/watch?v=1tRq8ExAHzk

RUBBING BUTCH T PEPPER INTO BOTH EYEBALLS *WARNING DO NOT TRY THIS*

Ted Burras (The Fire Breathing Idiot) cuts a Butch T pepper in half, massages it in and around his eyes and then eats the pepper. He is soon screaming in agony and is blinded for 70 minutes. 'That should only be a method of torture at Guantanamo Bay. It felt like rubbing sandpaper on my eyeballs as hard as I could.' This man truly is an idiot.

youtube.com/watch?v=T9LQiBhMiXM

THE SRIRACHA CHALLENGE

Extreme eater LA Beast (tagline 'I Gotta Go To The Hospital') proves what goes down must come up when he chugs three bottles of Huy Fong Foods Sriracha sauce in an astonishing three minutes. By the end, there's more red stuff being splashed around than in your average Tarantino movie.

youtube.com/watch?v=toJDo046mm4

CHILLIES ON SCREEN

From the ridiculous to the sublime, chillies make an appearance in everything from the grossest of gross-out comedies to the most refined of art-house flicks. So grab a box of chilli-flavoured popcorn, settle into your favourite chair and get ready for an amazing chilli-tastic viewing fest.

DUMB & DUMBER

In what is perhaps their finest moment on screen, Emmy award winner Jeff Daniels and double Golden Globe winner Jim Carrey eat 'atomic peppers' at Dante's Inferno restaurant in Mississippi then chug tomato ketchup and mustard in an attempt to ease the pain. They then stuff their rotund travelling companion's burger full of the chillies. When he passes out, Jim Carrey tries to administer CPR and mouth to mouth in a truly bizarre fashion. Why no Oscar?

CHOCOLAT

This is, according to the trailer, a 'sinfully delicious comic fable' that features Juliette Binoche making an entire village in rural France randy with her chilli-spiked chocolates. Worth watching for Johnny Depp's hilarious attempt at an Irish accent alone.

TAMPOPO

Do not see this movie hungry or at least make sure you're within five minutes of a ramen shop (better still, make the chilli beef ramen recipe on page 22 first). This Japanese 'ramen western' (no really, stick with it, it's wonderful) is a simple story of a cook's quest for the perfect ramen recipe that's told with lashings of humour, sex and pathos. The cooking and eating scenes will have your stomach growling.

EAT DRINK MAN WOMAN

Time, Chilli Heads, to get in touch with your sensitive side. This is a profoundly moving story about an emotionally crippled, ageing masterchef, Mr. Chu who shows his love for his three daughters by preparing exquisite banquets for them. If that's not enough to put you off watching it, it was made in Taiwan by acclaimed director Ang Lee (who later went on to direct the first Hulk movie) and is subtitled. But if it doesn't exactly sound your thing, bear with it, the cooking is fantastic, including the opening scene where Mr. Chu prepares a chilli with astonishing dexterity.

SRIRACHA - THE MOVIE

This documentary explores the phenomenon of the 'hipster's Tabasco', Sriracha sauce. It tells the story of David Tan and Huy Fong Foods, the legendary LA based company that produces the iconic rooster label Sriracha Hot Chili Sauce, including an interview with the great man himself, plus plenty of talking Chilli Heads.

CHILLI SONGS

Chillies have appeared throughout the history of the popular song, from 1930s blues and jazz to modern rock. Some of these chilli tunes are hot classics, others are a flaming mess. But they're all worth listening to, even if only for the yuks.

'CHILI DOG' BY JAMES TAYLOR

Sensitive 70s singer-songwriter type James Taylor claims that he wants you to 'spread some mustard upon his head' in this 96-second snatch of obscure MOR nonsense. Maybe the now-bald balladeer thinks the condiment might help restore his once luxuriant locks, the hot-headed old fool.

'CHILI SAUCE' BY THE TIME

This lame spoken-word 'comedy' song was written by Prince for his side project funk band The Time. By far the worst track on the 1984 *Ice Cream Castle* album, a gangster seduces a young lady in a restaurant to a slow-burning soul backing track and asks her to signal her acquiescence with the words 'chili sauce'. The listener is led to assume this is code for a particularly naughty version of sexy time.

'CHILI CON CARNE' BY THE REAL GROUP

The fact that this Swedish a cappella combo (they're not a 'real' group, are they? Real groups have drummers with bad personal hygiene and lead guitarists with drug problems) sing a recipe for chilli that includes the phrase 'don't forget the Mexican spices' over a Brazilian bossa nova beat is bad enough (see also Jamie Oliver singing a recipe for Indian curry in a West Indian accent at www.youtube.com/watch?v=0_KyYs0Ipy0) but writing a paean to one of the world's greatest dishes that's so bland, lightweight and lily-livered is simply unforgivable.

'CHILI SAUCE' BY LOUIS PRIMA

New Orleans-born big band leader Louis Prima is best known as the voice of King Louis in Disney's The Jungle Book, in which he sang the film's most famous song, 'I wanna be like you'. But his recording career lasted from 1934 right up until 1975, and includes numerous good-time numbers like this two-minute blast of trumpet-fuelled mambo fun that was used in a 2001 Adidas commercial.

'CHILI' BY KING CURTIS

American sax legend King Curtis lent his distinctive growling tone to many 1950s hits including 'Yakety Yak' by The Coasters and influenced Clarence Clemons of Bruce Springteen's E Street Band. This bluesy mid-tempo instrumental would make the perfect soundtrack to any chilli cooking session.

'THEY'RE RED HOT' BY ROBERT JOHNSON

Legend has it that Robert Johnson sold his soul to the devil on a Mississippi crossroads at midnight in exchange for the ability to play guitar. The 30s bluesman hardly played down the story with songs like 'Hellhound on my Trail' and 'Me and the Devil Blues', but this is an altogether more playful ditty. Ostensibly about a tall girl who sells hot tamales, it's not too difficult to find a more salty interpretation of lyrics like 'she got something good she got to bring home soon'.

'CAN'T STOP' BY RED HOT CHILI PEPPERS

Arguably the LA funk punkers' finest moment. Who could resist a song that includes the lines 'Can't stop, addicted to the shindig' or 'Go ask the dust for any answers, come back strong with fifty belly dancers'? And if you want to know where the Chili Peppers got their spiky rhythms and staccato guitar stylings from, give 'Entertainment' by Gang of Four a spin sometime.

HOW TO BECOME A CHILLI HEAD SAUCE BARON

You've been to the festivals, done the internet thing and maybe even formed your own club, but there's only one way to reach the top of the chilli head tree and that's by marketing your own chilli sauce. There are literally millions to be made from bottling your culinary creation, as Vietnamese-born entrepreneur David Tran has proved. Don't recognise the name? How about Huy Fong Foods? No, well you've almost certainly squeezed some of his Sriracha Hot Chilli Sauce over a burger or bowl of chilli. The Los Angeles-based company sold 20 million bottles of the distinctive rooster-branded sauce in 2012 alone.

Tran's story is an inspirational one. It began in 1980 with Tran grinding jalapeños by hand, mixing them with vinegar, sugar, salt and garlic, bottling the sauce and delivering them to local restaurants in an old van. Seven years later, demand for the sauce had increased so much that he transferred operations to a large factory. By the early 2000s, the Asian supermarket staple crossed over to the mainstream and was stocked in Walmart supermarkets and upmarket restaurants in America such as David Chang's Momofuku group.

But beware, if you do decide to follow in Tran's footsteps, you won't be the first to do so. A visit to a chilli festival, specialist chilli shop or even a quick look at peppers.com will reveal the Styx-like river of chilli sauce flowing around the world. If you want to get your hands on the big bucks, you need to make your version stand out from the thousands of competitors and be irresistible to your fellow Chilli Heads.

The first step is to decide what sort of sauce you want to make. Some of the main styles include single chilli variety sauces such as Chipotle, Jalapeño and Habañero; chilli pepper blends; Louisiana-style sauces (e.g. Tabasco); fruit based sauces and extra hot, or XXX, sauces. Try as many brands as you can to see what you like, including market leaders like Blair's Original Death Sauce (a blend of Habañero, Cayenne and Chipotle), Dave's Gourmet Insanity Sauce (launched in 1993, it was one of the first sauces to be made with capsaicin extract and rates around 180,000 SHU), Ca John's Hot Spots cayenne sauce, Marie Sharp's Habañero Pepper Sauce, Cholula Mexican-style hot sauce made with Piquin chillies and Ashley Foods' Mad Dog range of extra-hot sauces.

Next you need a killer recipe. You can make a sauce with just three ingredients – Tabasco contains just chillies, vinegar and salt – but you

can add complexity and depth with herbs, spices, fruits and vegetables. The crucial thing is to make something that appeals to your palate using your favourite chillies, and delivers the level of heat you can enjoy most. That way you'll have no problem convincing others that it's a hot prospect. Once you're up and running it's time to start expanding your range and tapping into the rest of the market.

Now the really fun part – naming your sauce. There's several ways you can go with this but the important thing is to tell a story. Firstly there's the 'does-what-it-says-on-the-tin' approach. Sriracha Hot Chilli Sauce might sound a bit dull but Tran has not only successfully co-opted a generic sauce style (named after the town of Si Racha in Thailand where the sauce was developed) but his Huy Fong Foods brand added interest by being named after the freighter that brought him to America as one of the 'Vietnamese boat people' refugees. The sauce even has a nickname, 'rooster sauce', after its logo that reflects Tran's birth in the Chinese Year of the Rooster.

Secondly there's the 'afterlife' genre that employs the words 'satan', 'devil', 'lucifer', 'hell', 'fire' ghost', 'death' and 'reaper' with exclamation marks and 'x's in various combinations. Feel free to add 'mad', 'insane', 'crazy' as well as 'hound', 'mamba', 'scorpion' and 'black' to the mix for best results e.g. Satan's Hell Fire Ghost Hound XXX Death Sauce!

Thirdly, you can abandon all good taste and head straight for the lowest common denominator with bottoms and swearing – 'ass', 'rectum', 'butt', 'sh*t' and 'f**k' are all essential here. But why stop there? Combine all three genres for the ultimate Chilli Head sauce name – 'Satan's Ancho Ass Ripping Sh*t Fire Ghost Mambo Scorpion Insane Zombie F**king Triple X California Reaper Death Sauce. With Garlic'.

Once you've got a kick-ass label designed for your sauce, marketing it is crucial. Entering it into major hot sauce awards such as the Scovies (scovieawards.com) or the Screaming Mimi's at the NYC Hot Sauce Expo (nychotsauceexpo.com) is a great way of drawing attention to your creation, because at this point you could still be making it from your kitchen at home (just make sure you're adhering to all your local government licensing and health department regulations before you start selling).

Use Twitter, Facebook, Instagram and other social media as sources of free advertising, hawk your wares around chilli festivals and events, and before you know it you could be the next David Tran.

SAUCE STAR MARK GEVAUX, A.K.A. THE RIB MAN, LONDON

'I used to be a butcher, but I lost my leg in an accident and couldn't be insured any more so I started selling baby back ribs at farmers' markets instead. I bought a disposable barbecue so I could cook samples and that's how I got into street food.

'I was looking for a hot sauce to serve with the ribs but couldn't find one that I liked, so I made my own. Holy F**k is my entry-level sauce (I had a competition on Twitter to name it and that won by a landslide. All the sauce names and label designs have come through my customers). It's Scotch Bonnet-based with Dorset Naga, tomatoes, a secret dry spice mix and olive oil. Scotch bonnets are amazing and they're the base of all of my sauces. I get Dorset Nagas

from Edible Ornamentals in Cambridge, the flavour and the heat totally complements and adds another dimension to my sauce.

'People kept asking for a hotter sauce and that's when Christ on a Bike was born, then I gradually increased the heat and made Holy Mother of God. Then they asked for a Naga sauce, so for Judas It's Scary Hot the ratio of Nagas and Scotch Bonnets is reversed.

'A lot of chefs have come down to my stall on Brick Lane, including Richard Turner of Hawksmoor and Mark Hix and both have the sauces in their restaurants. They bang on about it on Twitter and it makes other chefs want to try it.

'The press coverage started when people blogged about me. I put links on my website and then joining Twitter was the big turning point. Appearances on TV shows like Lorraine Pascale and Adam Richman, who loved my food and told everyone, didn't do me any harm. People come from Italy and France because they've seen me on the TV. Through my website I've had orders from across Europe, America, Canada, Malaysia, Ukraine and all over Russia. I'm now looking to get my brand in airports and railway stations in the UK. The next step is to get the sauces made in a factory for the wholesale side of things but I'll still make it myself for the stall.'

theribman.co.uk

THE TOP 10 MOST OUTRAGEOUS CHILLI SAUCE BRANDS

 Angry Cock Hot Sauce There's a picture of an annoyed chicken on the label. Well, what were you expecting? Made in Ohio with mostly Bhut Jolokia chillies, this sauce is bound to keep your pecker up.

 Butt Pucker: Professor Payne Indeass's XX Hot Sauce D'ya see what they did there? Pretty clever stuff, in a very dumb sort of way. Made in Florida with aged cayenne peppers.

 Carlsbad Arrogant Double Bastard Double Burn This Habañero-based hot sauce is made with 11 per cent proof Arrogant Double Bastard ale from the Stone Brewing Company in California, hence the name.

 Professor Phardtpounders Colon Cleaner Because farts are funny. They just are. Just to be clear, he's not a real professor and although the bottle looks vaguely medicinal, the sauce really isn't. Made in Florida with lots of mustard and Scotch Bonnets for plenty of poke.

Crazy Jerry's Biker Trash D.I.L.L.I.G.A.F. Habañero Garlic Hot Sauce The acronym stands for Do I Look Like I Give A Fandango and reflects sauce maker Crazy Jerry's aversion to Portuguese folk dance. Of course it doesn't, the F stands for... oh, just use your imagination. You won't have to think too hard about this sauce though, it's packed with flavour from roasted garlic, lemon juice and plenty of Habañero.

Dr. Assburn's All Natural Elixir Fire Roasted Habañero Pepper Sauce Dr. Assburn used to work in the field of gastroenterology until one day he realised his career choice was one of the most extraordinary cases of nominative determinism on record and gave it all up to make his range of sauces. That's not true, but what is undisputable is that this sauce is made in Florida from fire roasted Habañeros.

Kiss My Bhut Hot Sauce OK, so it's not that outrageous, but it is funny. Made with super-hot Bhut Jolokia of course.

Nuckin' Futs Hot Sauce Enjoy the spoonerism as you spoon some of this Tennessee hot sauce made with Habañeros all over your breakfast. Although frankly, you'd have to be nuckin' futs to do that.

This Sauce Tastes Like Sh*t Someone needs to have a word with the marketing department. This Habañero sauce from Delaware is an unappetising brown colour too. What were they thinking?

Weapons of Ass Destruction Hot Sauce There's nothing like a good pun, and this is nothing like etc etc. Bottom line? At least this Habañero sauce delivers in the heat department.

ULTIMATE CHILLI HEAD SAUCE

Your chilli sauce recipe should be as personal to you as the collection of drunk photos on your Facebook page. Like those photos, it should be something you wouldn't want your mum to get hold of. Not because it's a source of eternal shame and embarrassment (haven't you heard of privacy settings?) but because it's just Too Hot To Handle. So take the following recipe as a template and put your own personal stamp all over it. Don't like Jalapeños? Then substitute De Árbol. Prefer your sauce a bit more on the savoury side? Then reduce the amount of honey. This is a medium-hot sauce but feel free to use any insanely hot chilli you like, even reducing the amount of tomatoes and making up the weight in chillies if you're really serious about murdering your tastebuds.

INGREDIENTS
- 1 chipotle in adobo, plus 1 tbsp of the adobo sauce
- 1 lemon drop chilli
- 1 habañero chilli
- 2 Ancho chillies, re-hydrated in hot water for 20 minutes (1–2k SHU)
- 2 tsp Madras curry powder
- 1 onion, skinned and roughly chopped
- 400g (14oz) canned San Marzano tomatoes
- 1 roasted red pepper, skinned and de-seeded
- 3 tbsp honey
- 1 tbsp dark brown sugar
- 100ml (3½fl oz) cider vinegar
- 3 tbsp balsamic vinegar
- 3 garlic cloves, skinned, halved and any green central stalk removed
- 1 tsp thyme leaves
- Salt

MAKES ABOUT 600ML/21FL OZ (ENOUGH FOR 2 BOTTLES)

1 In a blender, combine the chipotle in adobo and sauce, all the other chillies, the curry powder, onion, tinned tomatoes, roasted red pepper, honey, dark brown sugar, cider vinegar, balsamic vinegar, garlic and thyme leaves.

2 Blend until completely smooth, transfer to a heavy bottomed pan (you'll risk burning the sauce if you use a cheap, thin one) bring to the boil, then simmer uncovered for 10 minutes, stirring to ensure the sauce doesn't catch. Season to taste with salt. Decant into sterilised bottles and store in the fridge for up to a month. Never let anyone in your house eat anything again without some of your wonderful homemade condiment on it.

Note If you want to make larger batches, just scale up the recipe by multiplying all the ingredients to the amount you want.

HOT WINGS

Created in 1964 at the Anchor Bar in Buffalo, New York (it's still open!), these spicy little nuggets of meat are truly irresistible and go down a treat with lashings of ice-cold beer. The recipe includes a method for making your own hot sauce but feel free to use a store-bought variety — Anchor Bar's own label sauce is available to buy online.

SERVES 4

INGREDIENTS

- Vegetable oil
- 450g (1lb) cayenne chillies
- 250ml (9fl oz) distilled vinegar
- 1 tsp celery salt
- 2 tsp paprika
- 1 tsp garlic powder
- 150ml (5fl oz) store-bought mayonnaise
- Vinaigrette (made by whisking 1 tsp mustard, 1 tbsp white wine vinegar, 60ml (2fl oz) rapeseed oil, salt and pepper)
- 100ml (3½fl oz) whipping cream
- 125g (4½oz) blue cheese, crumbled
- Squeeze of lemon juice
- 500g (1lb 2oz) chicken wings
- 125g (4½oz) butter
- Splash of Worcestershire sauce
- Pinch of cayenne
- Pinch of celery salt
- 1 garlic clove, finely chopped
- Salt and black pepper

1 For the hot sauce, lightly oil the chillies, place them in a single layer on a baking tray and roast in the oven at 200°C/400°F/Gas mark 6 until the skin blisters. Transfer to a bowl, cover with cling film and leave for 10 minutes. Using plastic gloves, remove the chilli skins. Place in a blender with the vinegar, celery salt, paprika and garlic. Strain, adjust the seasoning, then decant into a sterilised glass jar. Keep in the fridge.

2 For the blue cheese dressing, combine the mayonnaise, vinaigrette, cream and blue cheese in a bowl and mix until smooth. Season with salt, pepper and lemon juice. Set aside.

3 Joint the chicken wings, discarding the tips. Toss in 1 tbsp vegetable oil and 1 tsp salt and bake in a single layer on a rack over a roasting tin at 220°C/425°F/Gas mark 7 for 25 minutes or until crisp and golden.

4 Heat the butter in a pan, add 60–125g (2¼–4½oz) of the hot sauce (depending on how fiery you like it), along with the Worcestershire sauce, cayenne, celery salt, garlic and black pepper. Heat until you can smell the garlic, then add the cooked wings and toss to coat.

5 Pile onto a plate and serve with the blue cheese dressing, and for the genuine Anchor Bar touch, celery sticks on the side.

Mighty endorphin power ranger Super-hot chilli that causes a powerful rush of endorphins when consumed.

CHILLI HEAD SLANG

If you want to fit into any cult then you have to speak the lingo, and being a Chilli Head is no exception. Memorise the following words and phrases and scatter through your next chilli-related conversation if you really want to be recognised as part of the inner circle.

Chumbled Contraction of 'chilli-humbled', to be humbled by the heat of a chilli, e.g 'that jolokia proper chumbled me'.

Singing Johnny Cash
Suffering from the after-effects of excreting chillies, a reference to the country music legend's hit 'Ring of Fire', e.g. 'I shouldn't have put those Butch Ts in the chilli last night, my bum's singing Johnny Cash this morning.'

Lucifered
To overindulge in chillies and related products, e.g. 'I went to the chilli festival yesterday and got well Lucifered on Dave's Insanity.'

Placenta dispenser
Derogatory term for a Chilli Head who removes the insides of a chilli, the hottest part, before consuming or cooking with it, e.g. 'He won't be able to eat that 7 pot, he's a placenta dispenser.'

Scov'ed up
To own a large collection of hot sauces that equates to numerous Scoville units, e.g. 'have you seen his shelves? He's totally Scov'ed up'.

Chemeister
A contraction of *chemesthesis* (the chemical sensibility of the skin and mucous membranes to capsaicin) and *meister* (master), to have a high tolerance to chilli heat, e.g. 'did you see him down that Carolina Reaper? He is the chemeister'.

Face shower
To sweat profusely around the forehead and cheeks due to eating a chilli, e.g 'he really took a face shower with that one'.

GOURMET CHILLI WORLD

3

MAN VS CHILLI

WHERE TO EAT THE WORLD'S HOTTEST DISHES

BRICK LANE CURRY HOUSE, USA

Join American TV presenter Adam Richman in the Phall Hall of Fame at one of the five Brick Lane Curry House locations in New York (bricklanecurryhouse.com). Claimed to be the hottest curry in North America, Brick Lane's tandoori chicken phall is cooked by a chef wearing a gas mask so he doesn't choke on the fumes from 10 different types of hot seasoning including Habañeros and something dubious called white chilli powder which is almost certainly not ground white chillies. The finished product is said to be 60 times hotter than a jalapeño. You get a free bottle of beer and your picture on the website if you finish the 16oz (453g) serving. Big whoop.

BREMEN PATISSERIE, AUSTRALIA

At Bremen Patisserie, 302 West St, Umina Beach, New South Wales, Australia (bremenpies.net.au) you can sip on a cup of in-house roasted artisan coffee while you pick up a loaf of German Rye bread. Or why not make like customer Shaun Mallincon and shovel down a Naga Jolokia meat pie in 28 seconds flat. For this incredible feat, Shaun took away nothing less than a free plain meat pie. Just what he fancied tucking into in the ambulance on the way to the hospital, no doubt.

ENGINE INN, UK

A pub in a picture postcard Lake District village might seem an unlikely setting to eat one the UK's most scorching dishes. But the Engine Inn, Cark in Cartmel, Grange over Sands, Cumbria (engineinn.co.uk) is just a short walk from Gerald Fowler's Chilli Pepper Company where he grows the Naga Viper chillies used in the pub's signature super-hot curry that's served with pilau rice, mango chutney and a giant poppadom. Pop in for a plate, you never know, you might bump into the great man himself.

DE.LISH CHEESECAKE CAFE, USA

Take the heat eating challenge that defeated uber Chilli Heads Scott Roberts (scottrobertsweb.com) and Jerret Ulmer (heataddicts.com) at De.Lish Cheesecake Cafe, 1060 Saint Catherine Street, Florissant, Missouri (delishcheesecakes.com) where they make a special version of their foot long Cajun-style Inferno beef sandwich topped with Jalapeños and Habañeros and stuffed with Bhut Jolokia and Moruga Scorpion. The rules state you have to eat the sandwich within 30 minutes, you can't leave the table, and anything dropping from the sandwich to the plate has to be eaten. No water can be consumed in the first minute, then you can drink as much as you like. And if you're sick anywhere on the property, you pay the owner $20 to clean it up. Another failed (male) challenger described the subsequent stomach pains and difficulty breathing as being 'as close as I will ever come to being in labour'.

THE WORLD'S HOTTEST CUISINES ON A PLATE

THAI

This South East Asian culinary powerhouse has been so successful in exporting its hot, sour, salty and sweet dishes that many Brits will have had a Thai dish at their local pub. Essential flavours include fish sauce, palm sugar, coriander, lime juice and coconut milk.

Bird's Eye (100–225K SHU) Small, thin and either red or green with loads of heat and a floral aftertaste.

Pad Thai Stir-fried rice noodles with egg, tofu, shrimp, chicken and chilli.

INDIAN

We've all 'gone for an Indian', but there's so much more to the cuisine of the subcontinent than the admittedly delicious fare of the high-street curry house. India's seventeen states all have their distinctive styles, from the coconut and fish curries of Kerala in the South to biriyani (lamb and rice cooked in a sealed pot) from Lucknow in the North. Some of the numerous spices used include turmeric, cinnamon and cumin.

Kashmiri (30–50K SHU) Long, thin red chilli often sold dried. Adds vibrant colour as well as heat.

Vindaloo A pork curry from Goa in the West made with Kashmiri chillies.

PERUVIAN

Western foodies are only just cottoning on to this ancient cuisine. Zinging with citrus and chilli, it tastes as modern as you like and it's healthy too, based around fresh seafood, beans and superfoods like quinoa. Yes, they eat guinea pig, but call it by its Peruvian name, *cuy*, and you'll love its subtle gamey flavour. And don't forget the Pisco Sour, the frothy national drink that packs a punch made with Pisco (Peruvian brandy), egg white, lime juice, syrup and bitters.

Limo (30–50k SHU) 5–7cm (2–2½in) long and red, yellow, orange, purple or white in colour with a pronounced citrus flavour.

Ceviche The national dish of Peru, made with diced raw fish that's quickly marinated in 'tiger's milk' made with lime juice, salt and chilli.

MALAYSIAN

It's a mystery why the approachable, spicy food of this beautiful country hasn't caught on around the world to the extent of its near neighbours Vietnam and Thailand. Hot chilli sambals and pungent dried shrimp paste add bags of flavour to curries, noodles and rice. There's Chinese influence in *Nonya* dishes like laksa noodle soups, and buttery *roti canai* bread has an unmistakably Indian touch.

Cili padi (bird's eye), **cili merah** (cayenne), **cili kering** (dried cayenne)

Char kuey teow Stir-fried rice noodles with soy, chilli, prawns, belacan, bean sprouts, and egg.

MEXICAN

There's something about the exuberant salsas (a fresh condiment made from raw chopped tomatoes, onions, chilli and lime juice), punchy guacamole (spicy avocado dip) and fun finger food like tacos (folded or rolled soft tortillas with various fillings) that just says 'party time'. Or maybe that's the pitcher of margarita cocktail talking.

Chilli de Árbol (15–30K SHU)
Also known as bird's beak or rat's tail, these 5–7cm (2–2½in) long bright red chillies are similar to cayenne in heat but with grassy, nutty and acidic notes.

Mole A chicken or beef stew flavoured with bitter chocolate and a paste of chillies, garlic, nuts and seeds.

CHINESE

If you're looking for heat in China then you need to head south west to Sichuan province, famous for its mouth-numbing Sichuan peppercorns and extensive use of chillies in dishes like hot and sour wok-fried kung pao chicken with water chestnuts, peanuts, spinach and chilli sauce.

Facing heaven chilli (30–50K SHU) is a cone-shaped, medium-hot pepper that grows to between 3 and 6cm (1–2½in). Its name comes from the fact that it grows pointing upwards.

Ma Po Tofu 'Pockmarked Grandmother Tofu' is named after the old Chinese woman who originally served the dish in her restaurant (rude!). This fiery dish of wok-fried tofu and minced beef gets it heat from chilli bean paste (broad beans fermented with chilli and salt) and Sichuan peppercorns.

VIETNAMESE

The varied regional cuisine in this long strip of a country takes its cues from neighbouring China, Laos and Cambodia with fresh *goi* salads with papaya or grapefruit-like pomelo, *bánh xèo* (savoury rice flour and coconut pancakes), noodle soups and *goi cuon* (translucent vegetable and shrimp spring rolls). French colonial influences are evident in *bánh mì*, a baguette filled with sliced pork, pâté, *cha lua* (Vietnamese pork sausage), pickled carrots, coriander and of course chillies.

Bird's Eye (100–225K SHU) Small, thin and either red or green with loads of heat and a floral after-taste.

Pho Pronounced 'fur', this spicy beef noodle soup supposedly gets its name from the French dish of poached meats *pot au feu*. The consommé-like broth is garnished with spring onions, coriander and plenty of sliced chillies.

CARIBBEAN

A melting pot of immigrant influences from Spain, Africa, China and India has resulted in a collection of dishes like ackee and saltfish (salt cod sautéed with boiled ackee fruit, Scotch Bonnet chillies, tomatoes and spices) and rice and peas (rice and kidney beans cooked in coconut milk with more Scotch Bonnets) that have an identity all of their own.

Scotch Bonnet (150–325K SHU) This plump and stout green, yellow or red chilli is meant to resemble a Scottish Tam o' Shanter hat and has prodigious heat and a distinctive sweet flavour.

Jerk chicken Chicken marinated in Scotch Bonnets, thyme, ginger and allspice berries then barbecued and served with rice and peas.

KOREAN

This East Asian cuisine remains unfamiliar to many, but has a lot to recommend it to the curious Chilli Head. Firstly there's *gochujang*, a savoury, pungent fermented condiment made from red chilli, glutinous rice, fermented soyabeans and salt that's used to marinate meat and pep up salads, stews and soups. Then there's *kimchi*, the spicy fermented cabbage that's become a worldwide foodie favourite – you might have had some in your burger if you've been to a trendy restaurant recently.

Gochugaru is not a variety of chilli but Korean chilli flakes made from dried and ground Korean red chillies. Usually vibrant red in colour, coarse in texture and with a hot sweet flavour.

Bibimbap Rice topped with *namul* (sautéed roots, leaves and sprouts) gochujang, egg and sliced beef.

HOT TO TROT
WHERE TO FIND THE WORLD'S SPICIEST STREET FOOD

BANGKOK

Snacking between meals is not advised, unless you're in the Thai capital. Maximise your Chilli Head dining opportunities in this sprawling, thrilling city by taking advantage of hawkers' stalls that seem to occupy every street corner. Head to the world-famous Chatuchak market to watch green papaya expertly sliced into fine strips by hand and combined with dried prawns, peanuts, long green 'snake' beans, cherry tomatoes, lime and bird's eye chillies for a fiery but refreshing *sômtam* salad. Many stallholders will adjust the heat for tourists so make sure you let them know you like it hot.

LONDON

You'll find all manner of global dishes being served at spots like Kerb Street food market in Kings Cross including Mexican burritos and Thai style *sômtam*, but undisputed king of the London street food scene is Mark Gevaux, better known as The Rib Man (see feature on page 62). Arrive early on a Sunday at Brick Lane market for his legendary slow cooked American-style ribs and slather generously with one of his infamous naughtily named sauces including F**k Yuzu.

MALAYSIA

In the capital of Kuala Lumpur much of the street food has migrated to the modern malls, but you can still find authentically delicious dishes such as *kway teow* (beef noodles with chilli sauce) at the gourmet emporium at the swanky Pavilion Mall. But for a more earthy experience head to Penang Island,where you'll not only find sandy beaches but countless roadside hawker carts and open air hawker centres. The list of dishes available is bewildering but there is an excellent guide at penang-traveltips.com.

LIMA

Dozens of stalls surround Lima's central market, all offering slightly different versions of the national dish, ceviche – raw diced fish that's 'cooked' by being tossed in lime and chilli. But with the hot sun beating down and little evidence of refrigeration, you need to choose your meal carefully. Better perhaps to stick to a slighter less known but equally delicious option of anticuchos that's served all over the city, including the Lince and Surquillo districts. Okay, it's sliced beef heart, but beef heart marinated in garlic, cumin, vinegar, salt and aji panca (Peruvian red chilli) cooked over charcoal with more of the spicy marinade and served with sliced potatoes and chilli sauce; it tastes like the finest steak you've ever eaten, only better and far, far cheaper.

MEXICO

Even if you haven't visited Mexico City, you'll probably have eaten or even cooked *tacos*, one of its most famous *antojitos* (street food) dishes. For the real thing, make a beeline for El Huequito at Ayuntamiento 21 just south of the city centre for *tacos al pastora* made with chilli marinated, spit-roasted and finely sliced pork that's served in a rolled tortilla with onion and coriander.

GERMANY

The unholy alliance of German cured sausage and Indian curry sauce should be a culinary abomination. In reality, currywurst is deliciously addictive and ideal northern European street food, a warming hearty dish perfect for when the weather's being typically northern European. Berlin is the home of currywurst and Curry 36 on Mehringdamm in Kreuzberg is its most famous stall but the Currywurst Sepp stand on Ehrenstrasse in Cologne serves a great version, too with the sliced bratwurst sausage drowned in a thick Vesta-like curry sauce, dusted with curry and chilli powder and served with chips and lashings of tomato sauce and mayonnaise on the side.

SINGAPORE

With influences from China, Malaysia and India, Singapore's many hawker centres such as Lau Pa Sat Festival Market and Maxwell Food Centre aren't lacking in variety. Don't miss Indonesian-style *Ayam Penyet* (smashed chicken) that's fried, softened in a pestle and mortar and served with *sambal* (chilli paste); chilli crab (in-the-shell crab stir fried in chilli sauce). Or try *roti john*, the breakfast of champions that's made up of Indian bread fried with egg, beef or sometimes mutton and served with chilli sauce.

JAMAICA

If you want the best jerk chicken, then set a course for Boston Bay in Portland, Jamaica, home to an annual jerk festival. But year round, the sandy beach and surrounding roads are full of hungry surfers and sun seekers feasting on the chicken, pork and sausage that's marinated with Scotch Bonnet chilli, allspice berries, thyme and ginger, then cooked to tender smoky deliciousness over locally cut pimento wood in pits under corrugated iron sheeting and served with rice and peas (rice and kidney beans cooked in coconut milk).

THE SHOCKING TRUTH ABOUT CHILLI CON CARNE

Ah, chilli con carne! That familiar and comforting dish of beef, chilli and well, what exactly? If you're thinking 'beans and tomatoes, obviously' then think again. There are as many recipes for the dish as there are cooks and as we'll see, some truly bizarre regional variations.

People may point and laugh at you if you say chilli con carne is a Mexican dish, and sneeringly tell you that in fact it was created 150 miles (240 km) from the Mexican border in San Antonio, Texas in the early 18th century by immigrants from the Canary Islands. If that happens, just play your secret Chilli Head Lourdes Nichols joker card.

Born in Mexico City and author of *The Complete Mexican Cookbook*, Nichols wrote that although chilli con carne is not really a Mexican dish, its origins lay in Mexico. 'In all probability it was when Americans came over the border for Mexican food and were offered *mole de guajolote* (wild turkey in chilli and chocolate sauce) accompanied by fried beans and white rice that they were inspired to try something similar'.

The confusion over the exact origin of the dish was exacerbated by a certain Mrs Owen, who wrote what might just be the first ever printed recipe for chilli con carne in 1880 and proclaimed for some unknown reason that it was 'the national dish of Mexico'.

Mrs Owen's recipe more likely evolved from the stews made by Texas cowboys travelling to the California gold fields in the mid-19th century who took bricks of dried beef flavoured with chilli that they rehydrated in boiling water. A similar version was also concocted to feed Texas prisoners around the same time.

But it was the Chilli Queens, Latino women who sold a plate of chilli for a dime from colourful wagons parked on San Antonio's Military Plaza in the 1880s, that ensured chilli con carne would forever be associated with the city. By the turn of the 20th century, cheap chilli joints and parlours began springing up all over the western states of America, and during the depression years kept many people from starving to death.

In the 1920s Macedonian immigrant Tom (Athanas) Kiradjieff created the gastronomic car crash known as Cincinnati Style Chilli. The Greek restaurant he'd opened with his brother John was doing poorly as no one in Cincinnati was familiar with the cuisine. To boost business they came up with a version of chilli con carne made with Middle Eastern spices including cinnamon, cloves and allspice and served it with spaghetti and a mound of shredded cheddar cheese on top. Because there is literally no accounting for taste, the creation was a smash hit, and Empress Chilli is still going strong today along with numerous other imitators.

As any Texan will tell you, 'If you know beans about chilli, you know chilli ain't got no beans'. The recipe for 'original Texas-style chilli' in the landmark 1966 book *A Bowl of Red*, written by fourth generation Texan, newspaperman and chilli fanatic Frank X. Tolbert lists only beef, Ancho chillies, oregano, cumin, cayenne pepper,

Tabasco and garlic. The meat and spices are cooked in water and then thickened with *masa harina* (Mexican corn flour) with not even a tomato in sight.

Fine if you live in a cattle town like San Antonio, but elsewhere in the country where beef was more expensive, pinto beans helped bulk up what would otherwise have been a pricey dish to prepare. Beans became a contentious issue among chilli connoisseurs and the issue came to a head in 1967 in a chilli cook-off in the remote ghost town of Terlingua, Texas.

In the ultimate battle of the bean, Texas reporter Homer 'Wick' Fowler went head to head with New York humourist and author H. Allen Smith (1906–1976) who had written an article entitled 'Nobody Knows More About Chili Than I Do', claiming that Texans didn't know how to make proper chilli and, just to twist the knife in further, he included a chilli con carne recipe that contained beans. The competition turned out to be a damp squib, however, and was called a draw when one of the (Texan) judges spat out Smith's chilli, claiming his taste buds were 'ruint'. Terlingua is now home to two annual chilli festivals where the question of 'to bean or not to bean' is no doubt debated still.

ULTIMATE CHILLI HEAD CON CARNE

There are as many different versions of chilli con carne as there are cooks. For example, Texas chilli may or may not include tomatoes and never, ever has kidney beans in it. You can read more about the evolution of chilli con carne on page 86, so without further ado, here's how to make the ultimate chilli con carne for Chilli Heads. This will feed about six to eight, depending how hungry they are.

INGREDIENTS

- 2 tbsp sunflower oil
- 750g (1lb 10oz) pork shoulder, diced
- 1 large onion, chopped
- 4 large cloves of garlic, crushed
- 2 tsp ground cumin
- 1 tsp cayenne
- 2 tsp ground fennel seeds
- 1 tbsp smoked paprika
- 1 Ancho chilli, reconstituted in water and diced
- Fresh diced chillies, variety and quantity of your choice
- 500g (1lb 2oz) minced beef
- 500ml (17fl oz) good beef stock
- 400g (16oz) can chopped tomatoes
- 400g (16oz) can black-eyed beans
- 400g (16oz) can kidney beans
- 1 tsp or so of cocoa powder
- 2 tsp dried oregano
- Tabasco or chilli sauce

1 Cut the pork into dice. Heat 1 tbsp of the oil in a roomy pan and fry the pork in batches until browned. Set aside. Add a little more oil to the pan and gently fry the onion until soft.

2 Add the garlic to the pan and cook for 1 minute, then add the ground cumin, cayenne, ground fennel seeds, smoked paprika, Ancho chilli and fresh chillies (1 Jalapeño with seeds removed will suffice if you're feeding non-Chilli Heads!).

3 Fry everything for a minute or so and then add the minced beef. Stir until the beef is nicely browned, then add the beef stock, making sure you scrape up all the tasty residue from the bottom of the pan. Return the pork to the pan, and add the chopped tomatoes, black-eyed beans, kidney beans, cocoa powder, dried oregano and salt to taste. Add water or stock to cover the meat if necessary, then bring to the boil and simmer gently, partially covering with a lid for 2 hours or until the pork is tender. Adjust the seasoning with salt and Tabasco or your favourite bottled chilli sauce if you think it needs it.

4 Serve with rice and a cucumber, red onion, chilli and lime salsa on the side.

MEET THE WORLD'S HOTTEST CHEFS

RICK BAYLESS, FRONTERA GRILL, CHICAGO

WHY IS HE HOT? Brought authentic Mexican cuisine to the US with Frontera Grill in 1987, then opened Topolobampo two years later, one of the first fine dining Mexican restaurants in America. He now runs seven restaurants in the city and has presented 10 seasons of his *Mexico – One Plate at a Time* TV show.

MUST ORDER *Carne asada*, Ancho chilli-marinated grilled rib-eye steak with black beans and avocado

MEXICAN

rickbayless.com

DAVID CHANG, RESTAURANT: MOMOFUKU, NEW YORK

WHY IS HE HOT? Chang's decade-old New York-based Momofuku restaurant group made its name serving Chinese/Japanese-style steamed pork buns with Sriracha chilli sauce. Chang's empire now stretches to Sydney, he publishes his own *Lucky Peach* food magazine and fronts the *Mind of a Chef* TV series.

KOREAN JAPANESE CHINESE

MUST ORDER *Bo ssäm*, lettuce wraps with slow-roasted pork shoulder, oysters, kimchi and spicy *ssäm* sauce

momofuku.com

DAVID THOMPSON, NAHM, BANGKOK

WHY IS HE HOT? Australian-born Thompson is a world authority on Thai cuisine and his book *Thai Food* is the definitive work on the subject. A meal of his deliciously fiery but refined food at his uber-swanky restaurant in Bangkok's hip Metropolitan hotel is a treat not to be missed.

MUST ORDER Minced prawns with shallots, young chillies, coriander, fresh vegetables and smoked pork

comohotels.com

KARAM SETHI, RESTAURANT: GYMKHANA, LONDON

WHY IS HE HOT? This modern upmarket Indian restaurant opened in 2013 to an orgy of rave reviews, propelling Sethi into London's top echelon. The *Evening Standard* described Gymkhana's Raj-inspired menu with dishes like *kid methi keema* (minced goat curry) with green chilli as 'magnificent'.

MUST ORDER Suckling pig vindaloo

gymkhanalondon.com

GASTÓN ACURIO, ASTRID Y GASTON, LIMA

WHY IS HE HOT? With 44 restaurants around the world, Acurio has single-handedly made Peruvian cuisine globally fashionable. The 29-course tasting menu at his flagship Astrid y Gaston restaurant that he opened in 1994 with his wife Astrid and now rated among the world's 50 best by *Restaurant* magazine is a culinary journey through Peru.

MUST ORDER Ceviche of octopus and squid with giant Peruvian corn kernels, fried plantains and yellow Aji chilli sauce

astridygaston.com

HOW TO BE A
CHILLI CONNOISSEUR

With thousands of varieties of chillies available, you need to keep track of what you'd love to eat over and over and what you'd never let pass your lips again. So why not make like a wine lover. That doesn't mean wearing a cravat and opening a bottle of claret at eleven in the morning, but keeping your own tasting notes. Wine aficionados note the appearance, aroma and taste of every bottle they open and give it an overall rating. You can apply the same method to fresh chillies (and with a little tweaking, to chilli sauces too). Take a few seconds to note down your thoughts in a book or on a spreadsheet and before you know it you'll be a walking Chilli Head encyclopedia.

First write down the chilli's name and find out where it was grown and how it rates on the Scoville scale. How does it look – is it short and stubby or long and slender, is the skin smooth or stubbly? Note the colour – chillies can be shades of red, green, yellow, orange, brown, purple and even black. Cut the chilli open and note how much placenta there is inside (this will affect how hot the chilli is).

Give the chilli a sniff and think about what it reminds you of – is it citrus, like a lemon or floral, like smelling a rose? Bite into the chilli (or eat it whole, making a note of how much of the chilli you consumed) and concentrate on the flavours in your mouth. Are they bitter, sweet or sour? Now the heat, is it an instant blast that dies away quickly or does it grow in intensity over time? Where do you feel the heat – on your tongue, at the back of the throat, is the roof of your mouth on fire or are your gums glowing?

Record any other effects like sweating, runny nose, tearing and coughing. If you've eaten a whole super-hot chilli, did it give you stomach cramps or any problems in the toilet department?

Now's the time to rate the chilli overall. Taking into account all the aspects of the chilli you've just assessed, give it a marking – that could be one to five stars, a score out of ten or anything else that makes sense to you – and say in one line why you loved or hated it. Congratulations, you are now an official Chilli Head connoisseur. Maybe you could wear that cravat – just make sure it's got chillies on it though.

FIVE CHILLIES TO COOK WITH

Believe it or not, chillies can blow your mind with something other than heat. Switched-on chefs know about the special varieties of our favourite fruit that offer smoky, sweet, aromatic, citric and floral notes to dishes. Sure, they pack heat too, just not so much that it overshadows their more subtle qualities. Even the most dedicated heat-seeking Chilli Head will admire what these babies bring to the table.

Cayenne The most commonly used dried chilli in the world. In its powdered form it pops up in everything from BBQ rubs to the French sauce *rouille* that's served with fish soup. The Chinese use whole dried cayenne chillies in Sichuan-style stir fries, and in India they are often quickly fried in hot oil along with other spices to make what's called a *tarka* which is then poured over lentil dals or cooked vegetables.

Poblano The most popular chilli in Mexico, it looks like a green bell pepper but has a strong pepper flavour and a kick to it. Serve it roasted, stuffed with cheese, meat or vegetables then battered and deep-fried with some salsa on the side for a classic chilli *rellenos*. When dried, it becomes the mild Ancho with hints of raisin, stone fruit and coffee flavours and an essential ingredient in authentic Texas-style chilli con carne.

Chipotle In its fresh form as Jalapeño (the variety you're most likely to pick up at the supermarket labelled simply as red or green chilli), this chilli is all about moderate heat. But dried and smoked it mutates into a complex little brute with concentrated smoky tones that adds body to Mexican dishes.

Amarillo Fruity and aromatic with a mild pepper flavour, this orange-coloured chilli is one of the most important ingredients in Peruvian cooking. Like a powered-down version of a Scotch Bonnet, it's used fresh or dried and ground and found in dishes like *Papas a la Huancaina* (boiled yellow Peruvian potatoes in a fresh cheese and chilli sauce).

Banana chilli Long and yellow, hence the name, these mild chillies are used in Thai salads and stir fries. Chargrilling brings out their natural smoky flavour.

CEVICHE

Ceviche is the national dish of Peru in South America, but the low-cal combination of fresh fish, lime juice and plenty of chilli is making it increasingly popular across the globe. Because the only 'cooking' the fish gets is during its short bath in the marinade, where the citric acid denatures the flesh (i.e. the cell structure of the fish proteins are broken down by the acid, making them softer), you need the freshest fish possible, so visit your local fishmonger rather than a supermarket for this recipe.

The simplest and best ceviche I've tasted was made by chef Javier Wong at his restaurant Chez Wong (it really is in his house) in Lima, the capital city of Peru where he expertly fillets then dices the flesh of a large and very fresh sole, adds cooked octopus, salt, lime juice, sliced red onion and a twist of black pepper and serves it immediately with a pot of diced Peruvian Rocoto chillies on the side.

SERVES 4

INGREDIENTS

- Juice of 8 limes
- Thumb-sized piece of fresh ginger, sliced
- Small bunch of coriander (leaves and roots separated)
- 1 garlic clove, crushed
- 1 red onion, finely sliced
- 500g (1lb 2oz) firm white-fleshed fish of your choice (royal bream, sea bass or sole is perfect), skinned, filleted and diced
- Diced chillies of your choice, to serve
- Salt and pepper

1 Ceviche is usually made with tiger's milk, but don't bother popping down to your local zoo with a bucket as it's actually just flavoured lime juice. Make by combining the lime juice, ginger, coriander roots and garlic. Infuse for 10 minutes, then strain into a bowl.

2 To complete the dish, place the onion in a bowl with the fish. Add the tiger's milk and leave to infuse for 1–5 minutes, depending on the size of the diced fish (there is no harm in serving the dish immediately, the fish will just have a more sashimi-like texture). Stir in the coriander leaves and one diced chilli of your choice. Season with salt and pepper, divide the ceviche between 4 plates, adding enough of the tiger's milk to moisten the dish but not drown it, and serve immediately with ice-cold beer and more diced chilli on the side.

CHILLI CHEESE FRIES

Haute cuisine it ain't, but there is simply nothing better than an enormous bowl of chilli cheese fries. You can just make them with canned chilli, frozen chips, slices of American Jack cheese and some fresh or pickled sliced chillies but here's a recipe for a slightly more labour-intensive version that pays dividends in the flavour department. If you've already made a spare batch of Ultimate Chilli Head Con Carne (see page 90) and have some Ultimate Chilli Head Sauce (see page 66) in your fridge then you are way ahead of the game. This will feed four generously.

SERVES 4

INGREDIENTS

- 4 large baking potatoes
- 2 tbsp vegetable oil
- 25g (1oz) butter
- 25g (1oz) flour
- 2 tsp American mustard
- 500ml (17fl oz) whole milk
- 200g (7oz) really good mature cheddar cheese (Montgomery if you can get it)
- Half quantity Ultimate Chilli Head Con Carne (see page 90)
- Chopped fresh or pickled chillies of your choice
- Ultimate Chilli Head Sauce (see page 66) or other chilli sauce, to serve
- Salt and pepper

1 Cut the potatoes in half and then each half into 4 wedges. Toss with salt, pepper and the vegetable oil and bake in the oven at 180°C/350°F/ Gas mark 4 for 25 minutes or until golden. When the chips are cooked, remove from the oven and increase the heat to 220°C/425°F/Gas mark 7.

2 Meanwhile, make the cheese sauce by melting the butter in a heavy bottomed pan. Add the flour and stir until well combined and golden. Add the mustard, then gradually stir in the milk. Bring to the boil, then simmer very gently for 20 minutes, stirring regularly to prevent the sauce catching. Off the heat, stir in the Cheddar until melted. Season and set aside.

3 Heat up the chilli con carne. When the chips are cooked, transfer them to a large baking dish, top with the chilli con carne, scatter over chopped chillies and pour over the cheese sauce. Put the dish in the hot oven and heat until the cheese bubbles and begins to turn brown. Serve with a green salad, and some chilli sauce on the side.

PORK VINDALOO

Beloved staple of the high-street curry house, the real thing as cooked in India is a very different beast from the fiery hot concoction known in the UK. Originating 400 years ago when Goa in West India was a colony of Portugal (it only came under Indian rule in 1961), the name is derived from the Portuguese for wine, *vinho*, and garlic, *alhos*.

Its most distinctive characteristic is not chilli heat but a relatively mild masala spice mix and vinegar, probably indicating that the wine originally used was soured stuff. So to make this more Chilli Head-friendly, what follows is a mash-up of the authentic and 'British' versions of the dish. Feel free to ramp up the chilli content to suit your palate.

SERVES 6

INGREDIENTS

- 2 tbsp ghee or vegetable oil
- 1 large onion, finely sliced
- 12 fresh curry leaves
- 1 tbsp garlic paste and 1 tbsp ginger paste (store-bought, or make your own by blending fresh garlic and ginger)
- 2 fresh cayenne chillies, or any chilli of your choice, finely chopped
- 1 tbsp cumin powder
- 1 tsp turmeric
- 1 tbsp coriander powder
- 2–3 tbsp chilli powder
- 1 tbsp paprika
- ½ tsp fenugreek (optional)
- 1 tsp cayenne
- 2 tsp garam masala
- 400g (16oz) can chopped tomatoes
- 2 tbsp cider vinegar
- 800g (1lb 12oz) pork shoulder, diced
- 2 large potatoes, diced

1 Heat the ghee or oil in a large pan and fry the onion over a medium heat until nicely browned. Add the curry leaves, garlic and ginger paste and cook for 2 minutes, stirring all the time until aromatic.

2 Add the chillies, cumin powder, turmeric, coriander powder, chilli powder, paprika, fenugreek (if using), cayenne and garam masala and fry until aromatic. Add the chopped tomatoes and vinegar and bring to the boil. Add the pork and bring back to the boil. Reduce to a simmer and cook gently for about 30 minutes. Add the potatoes, bring back to the boil, reduce to a simmer and cook for a further 30 minutes or until the pork and potatoes are tender. Serve with Basmati rice, cooked as per the packet instructions.

4

THE CHILLI
CULTIVATOR

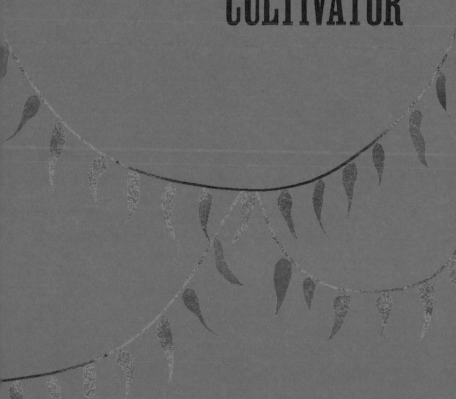

THE CHILLI GARDENER'S TOOL KIT

No serious Chilli Head can resist the urge to propagate their own crop of the blessed fruit. The good news is that many varieties of chillies are one of the easiest things you could choose to grow and you can do it with very little equipment or expense. You can start with a pot on a shelf in the conservatory or kitchen.

For absolute beginners, there are some great value grow-your-own-chilli kits available. The South Devon Chilli Farm's (southdevonchillifarm.co.uk) One Pot kit includes a plastic pot and saucer, a propagator lid, compost, liquid plant food, Apache F1 chilli seeds and instructions.

Source your seeds from your local nursery or DIY store or get more specialist varieties from online companies like Simpson's Seeds (simpsonsseeds.co.uk). If you fancy trying your hand at a tricky super-hot variety, you can order Naga Viper seeds from Gerald Fowler's Chilli Pepper Company (chileseeds.co.uk).

All the basic equipment you need to grow your first plants is detailed on the next page, but if you want to grow a larger crop then you're going to have to splash some cash. Chillies thrive on heat and light so a polytunnel or greenhouse is essential for cooler climates. Get the largest you can afford and make sure you choose toughened glass for your greenhouse, especially if you have football-loving offspring.

If you've got lots of plants, a self-watering system from a company like Auto Pot (autopot.co.uk) is a good idea. Low maintenance, soil-free Hydroponic Nutrient Film Technique kits (available from greenhousepeople.co.uk and other stockists) are ideal for chilli plants and will provide larger crops in double quick time. Finally, LED growing lights from suppliers such as Led Hydroponics (ledhydroponics.co.uk) will encourage growth when natural light is harder to come by.

HOW TO GROW YOUR OWN CHILLIES

If you think the first step to cultivating chillies is to move to the Caribbean, then think again – some of the hottest chillies on the planet are grown in gloomy old northern England.

As well as being fun and hugely rewarding, growing your own will save you money and give you ready access to some of the more obscure and hottest varieties of chillies you'll never find on your supermarket shelves and that are tricky to buy fresh even on the internet.

Once you get really proficient, you could create your own brand new strain of chilli that you can modestly name after yourself – fame at last. Even if your middle name isn't 'greenfingers' and you've killed an office pot plant or two through neglect, don't worry, your gardening salvation lies with the noble *Capsicum annuum* (see, you already know the Latin name for the common chilli.).

GROWING A CHILLI - STEP BY STEP

1 **Buy your seeds** You'll find seeds at your local DIY/garden store but if you want any other than the common varieties, head for specialist websites like www. chileseeds.co.uk. Some varieties are easier to cultivate than others, so give yourself the best chance of success first time out and go for Cherry Bomb or Ring of Fire. You can harvest seeds from fresh chillies; just remember to wear gloves and for the hottest varieties, eye goggles, as the capsaicin oil in the chilli 'placenta' or membrane will sting like mad if it makes contact with sensitive areas of the face and body. Dry them in an airing cupboard for a week or two before use.

2 **Germinate the seed** This is the first stage of your seed turning into a plant; you basically want it to sprout. You can accelerate the process by putting the seeds between sheets of damp kitchen roll in a plastic container and keeping it somewhere warm, but the easiest thing to do is put them directly into soil. You can buy a fancy propagator from your garden store but a cheap food storage container with some holes punched in the base for drainage will do just as well.

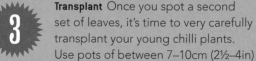

Sow the seeds a few centimetres apart on top of the soil and then just cover with more soil. Water lightly to moisten but don't drown the poor things. Put them somewhere warm (on top of the fridge), cover with cling film and wait a few weeks or so, watering if necessary. Check daily and as soon as you see signs of growth above the surface, your chillies will need light to continue to grow so move them, still in their container, to somewhere warm and bright in the house but out of direct sunlight. A conservatory would be great but a windowsill above a radiator is also perfect. Keep the soil moist.

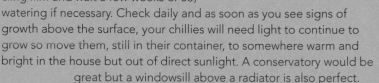

3 **Transplant** Once you spot a second set of leaves, it's time to very carefully transplant your young chilli plants. Use pots of between 7–10cm (2½–4in) for each seedling and fill them with moist compost. Rather than uprooting the plant, transfer it to the pot with the propagation soil still surrounding the delicate root system so you don't damage it. In addition to watering lightly, feed the plant with fertilizer or liquid tomato feed. As the plants continue to grow, you'll need to replant to bigger pots and once they reach about 20cm (8in) in height, tie them to canes in the pot for support.

4 **Pollination** When your plants flower, it's time to get excited – you're only a step away from your first home-grown chilli! Now it's time to act like a bee. No, that's not an excuse to run around the living room flapping your arms and making an annoying buzzing sound – you're going to have to get up close and personal with your plants. Use your finger, or a cotton bud if you prefer, and rub the stamen of each flower, thereby spreading the pollen as you go and maximising the number of chillies that will eventually grow.

5 **Harvest** Continue to care for the plants as before, watering lightly and fertilizing and your chillies will appear. Remove the first fruits while they are green, this will encourage the plant to produce more fruit for longer. Allow all subsequent fruit to fully ripen. You can transfer your plants to the garden once the weather is warm enough but find them a sheltered and sunny spot.

GROWING TIPS FROM A PROFESSIONAL

In 1996, Sarah Wain, Garden Supervisor at West Dean Gardens, West Sussex, became one of the first growers of multiple varieties of chilli in the UK when she cultivated 75 different plants including Tabasco, Serrano and Jalapeño, leading to an appearance that year on the BBC's *Gardeners' World* TV show. She currently grows in excess of 250 varieties including rare and obscure types such as Sweet Wrinkled Old Man, Medusa and Black Olive, which form the highlight of the annual West Dean Chilli Fiesta, one of the UK's premier chilli festivals.

 It is possible to grow chillies outside in the south of England in a favourable year in a sun-soaked position at the base of a south-facing wall. But a well-protected patio, a glasshouse, conservatory or windowsill is far more reliable.

 Choose varieties from the *Capsicum annuum* species, which are generally the fastest to germinate and the most robust. You can delay sowing them until spring when it naturally warms up and still get a crop by the end of the year. Hungarian Hot Wax is very reliable and gives you chillies that you can use as spice, grill, pickle or stuff. It looks glorious as it ripens from yellow to orange and then scarlet orange. Sparkler is another fantastic variety with masses of skinny centimetre-long chillies, perfect if you're making your own curry paste and you'll only need one or two plants.

✳ Habañero, Scotch Bonnets and Carolina Reapers are *Capsicum chinense* and they tend to be more erratic and take longer to germinate, grow, flower and fruit so start them earlier in the season in early spring with your thermostat set at 25° Celsius (77° Fahrenheit) and grow them for a couple of months under grow lights.

✳ Depending on the variety you're growing, you could get the fruits from between late spring through to autumn.

✳ To promote bushy growth, when the plants are about 20cm (7¾in) high, break the tip off above a pair of leaves; the buds below the break will form branches and you'll get a much bushier plant.

✳ Pot your plants in free-draining soil with a good potting mix. I use a combination of John Innes and multipurpose. I grow them in 5 litre (8¾ pints) terracotta pots for the more robust varieties, the smaller varieties will be quite happy in a 2 litre (3½ pints) pot.

✳ My personal favourite variety is called Michael's Magic, a Habañero type given to me by a serviceman in the armed forces who found it in a marketplace somewhere on his travels. It's early fruiting and very reliable but you can only buy it if you come to the West Dean Chilli Fiesta.

HOT ON YOUR HEELS

JOIN THE RACE TO GROW THE WORLD'S HOTTEST CHILLI

Since 1994 and the cultivation by Frank Garcia of GNS Spices of the half-a-million Scoville unit-rating Red Savina Habañero in Walnut, California, the race has been on to land the super-hot chilli record. With an ever-increasing market for hot chillies and sauces, the financial advantages of growing the world's hottest chilli are obvious, but current Guinness World Record holder 'Smokin' Ed Currie of the Pucker Butt Pepper Company in South Carolina has an entirely different motivation for producing the Carolina Reaper, which at its peak tops out at 2.2 million SHU.

As a survivor of both skin and thyroid cancer, Currie says he's been symptom-free since he started eating between eight and 12 fresh chillies a day. Currie shares his research data with the medical fraternity in the hope of one day finding a chilli-based cure for cancer. But even securing a world record takes a lot of time, effort and dedication, as Currie explains.

'Every year I take twenty peppers and breed each one with all the others. I usually use the cross-pollination method. We've found that one in ten produces a new variety or "phenotype" that's worthy of working with. One of those was a Naga from Pakistan crossed with a Habañero from St Vincent in the Caribbean and what came out was a chilli that literally made me dizzy, and that became the Carolina Reaper.'

But Guinness won't bestow a record on a single chilli. Any new phenotype has to be proven to be stable, and that's where things get a bit more complex.

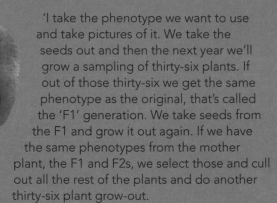

'I take the phenotype we want to use and take pictures of it. We take the seeds out and then the next year we'll grow a sampling of thirty-six plants. If out of those thirty-six we get the same phenotype as the original, that's called the 'F1' generation. We take seeds from the F1 and grow it out again. If we have the same phenotypes from the mother plant, the F1 and F2s, we select those and cull out all the rest of the plants and do another thirty-six plant grow-out.

'I use greenhouses and if I'm aggressive I can do that three times a year, un-aggressive we can do it twice because plants take about one hundred and twenty days to mature. We do that over and over again until we get the eighth generation grow-out. I work with a botanist, a horticulturalist, a biologist and a chemist at a university, and together we decide if at that point it's a stable plant.'

Data released in 2009 from one of the two separate three-year studies carried out on the Carolina Reaper showing an average of 1.47 million SHU over a three-year period caused an uproar in the Chilli Head community.

'I grew for chilli sauce makers but other than that, no one really knew who I was,' says Currie. 'At the time the hottest thing in

Guinness was about 1.2 million SHU so over the next three years I went back and forth with the record book. They had me do a whole bunch of different things and they changed their rules as far as peppers went during that time. But they finally gave me the record in 2013.'

But that's not the end of the story. Driven by his passionate belief in the medical benefits of super-hot chillies, Currie continues on his quest to produce ever-hotter chillies. 'This year we've got eleven hundred different kinds of super-hot chillies. We've already produced Carolina Reapers that register 2.5 million SHU and we've got nine crosses that are all testing out at over 2 million SHU. When one of those becomes stable, we'll submit that to Guinness and then keep on releasing them. If my research is correct we'll be able to generate plants that average out at 3.8 million SHU and at peak get close to 5 million SHU.

'But the goal is to give them to chemists and biologists and oncologists so they can get them into a nutrient scheme for cancer patients. Most capsinoids contain a key that fits into a cancer cell that will kill it, it's the delivery method that they don't have down yet. If I can be a small part in God's masterplan I'm going to keep on doing it. People say I'm obsessed but I'm trying to change the world.'

THE HEAT MAP – THE WORLD'S BIGGEST CHILLI PRODUCERS

CHINA 16,023,500

MEXICO 2,379,736

TURKEY 2,072,132

INDONESIA 1,656, 615

UNITED STATES 1,064,800

SPAIN 1,023,700

EGYPT 650,054

NIGERIA 500,000

ALGERIA 426,566

ETHIOPIA 402,109

Figures (in tons) are for annual production in 2012 and sourced from the Food and Agriculture Organisation of the United Nations Statistics Division

NIGHT OF THE CHILLI HEADS
A CHILLI HEAD RAP

Dawn of the Chilli Heads, prophets of heat,
Taking chilli gospel to the streets,
Scoville units are our stock in trade,
Bringing you the fire that never fades.

Scorpion, Viper, Naga, Reaper,
If you don't know what that means, we're gonna teach ya,
Building up resistance day by day,
Super hot chillies never make us pay.

Day of the Chilli Heads, cradle to grave,
Capscaicin heat is all we crave,
Chugging down Insanity like cold beer,
Chewing Bhut Jolokias with nothing to fear.

Growing hybrids in large amounts,
Cooking chilli sauce by the ounce,
Reviewing pods on my YouTube channel,
I've got more fire than you can handle.

Night of the Chilli Heads, now it's our turn,
What we know you'll burn to learn,
Turn up the heat, pay the devil his due,
Now you're rocking with the Chilli Head crew.

THAI GREEN CHICKEN CURRY

Thai green curry can't be too far behind chicken tikka masala as one of the UK's favourite hot dishes. It's perfect Chilli Head food too; make it as searingly hot as you like and there's still plenty of delicious complexity from ingredients like galangal (a type of ginger), sweetness from palm sugar and soothing coconut milk to balance the whole thing out. If you're a keen cook, make your own chilli paste as per the instructions opposite (you may have to visit your local Asian supermarket to find some of the ingredients, or order them online), it will taste fantastic and keep in the fridge for a few weeks. Alternatively, just buy ready-made chilli paste (that's what many Thais do, albeit fresh from their local daily market) – Blue Dragon is good and widely available.

SERVES 4

INGREDIENTS

- 3 tbsp green Bird's Eye chillies
- Pinch of sea salt
- 1 tbsp chopped galangal
- 2 tbsp chopped lemongrass
- 1 tbsp chopped kaffir lime zest
- 1 tbsp chopped coriander
- 2 tbsp chopped shallots
- 2 tbsp chopped garlic
- 1 tsp Thai shrimp paste
- 150ml (5fl oz) coconut cream
- 1 tbsp palm sugar
- 1 tbsp fish sauce
- 400ml (16oz) can light coconut milk
- 500g (1lb 2oz) skinless chicken breast, diced
- 250g (9oz) sugar snap peas, cooked in fast boiling water for 1 minute and drained
- Thai holy basil leaves, to serve
- Sliced long red Thai chillies or other chilli of your choice, for garnish

1 If you have a large pestle and mortar, grind the chillies to a paste – a pinch of sea salt will help the process. Then grind the galangal, lemongrass, lime zest, coriander, shallots, garlic and shrimp paste. Alternatively, put all the ingredients in a blender with a teaspoon of water for 3–4 minutes.

2 Bring the coconut cream to the boil in a large pan. When the oil begins to separate out, add 2–3 tbsp of your paste to the pan (depending on how hot you want your curry) and stir-fry for a few minutes until it releases its aromas. Add the palm sugar and fish sauce and stir well. Pour in the coconut milk and bring to a simmer. Add the chicken and simmer for 5 minutes. Add the sugar snap peas and simmer for a further 3 minutes or until the meat is cooked through and the peas are tender.

Divide between 4 bowls and garnish each with torn Thai holy basil leaves and sliced chillies. Serve with Jasmine rice cooked as per the packet instructions.

DONER KEBABS

After a night out, what self-respecting Chilli Head can ignore the siren call of the kebab shop? Large doner, salad, chilli sauce and extra pickled chillies is what you need. But be honest, the anticipation is often better than the reality, with greasy flavourless meat (what the heck are those rotating elephant's feet made of anyway?), cardboard pitta and underpowered chilli sauce. Far better to make them yourself at home and eat one to line your stomach before you go out rather than burn the house down trying to knock one up at two in the morning. Making your own pitta is easy but shop-bought are fine too.

INGREDIENTS

SERVES 4

- 500g (1lb 2oz) strong white bread flour
- 1 tbsp fast-acting yeast
- 150ml (5fl oz) tepid water
- 150ml (5fl oz) plain yoghurt
- Good pinch of salt
- 2 tbsp olive oil
- 500g (1lb 2oz) lamb mince
- 1 garlic clove, minced
- 1 tbsp plain flour
- 2 tbsp rapeseed oil
- 1 tbsp ground cumin
- 1 tsp ground fennel seeds
- 1 tsp cayenne
- 1 tsp dried oregano
- 1 tsp dried mint
- 1 egg, beaten
- Sliced white cabbage, red onion and chillies, dressed with lemon juice
- Plain yoghurt, to serve (optional)
- Your favourite hot sauce, to serve

1 Make the pitta dough by combining the flour, yeast, water, yoghurt, salt and olive oil in the bowl of a food mixer. Using the dough hook and the slowest setting, knead the mixture for 5 minutes or until you have a smooth dough. Alternatively, combine the ingredients in a bowl, then turn out onto an oiled work surface and knead by hand for 5–10 minutes. Return to the bowl, cover and leave to rise for 30 minutes in a warm and draft-free place. Divide into 8 balls, and roll out into oval shapes. Cook in the oven on pre-heated baking trays at 230°C/450°F/Gas mark 8 for a couple of minutes until puffed up. Any leftover pittas can be frozen.

2 To make the kebab meat, combine the lamb mince, garlic, flour, rapeseed oil, ground cumin, ground fennel seeds, cayenne, dried oregano, dried mint and egg in a bowl. Spread the mixture over a shallow 24cm (9½in) baking tray that's been lined with greaseproof paper and lightly oiled. Place under a medium-hot grill until browned. Remove from the grill, invert the pan onto a board then return to the baking tray, cooked-side down. Grill until browned. Turn out onto the board again and slice.

3 Reheat 4 pittas in a toaster if necessary, fill each with some of the meat, top with the salad, a spoon of yoghurt, if using and lashings of hot sauce (Maggi hot and sweet would be perfect).

CHILLI JOKES

Man goes into a diner in Texas, sits at the counter and orders chilli con carne. The waitress tells him, 'We're sold out, the guy next to you got the last bowl.'

Disappointed, he asks for a coffee and checks his phone to find the nearest alternative place for the chilli he's set his heart on. After a short while, he notices the man sitting next to him has finished eating but the chilli appears to be untouched. 'Are you going to eat that?' asks the chilli-craving man, and the other guy tells him no and please go ahead and take it.

Now hungry as hell, the man attacks the bowl with relish, chowing down on the long-desired chilli. He finishes about half then spots the body of a dead mouse in his food. Disgusted, he throws up the chilli back into the bowl.

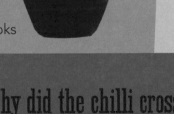

The other guy looks over to the now distressed man and with a smirk says, 'That's about as far as I got too.'

Why did the chilli cross the Peruvian road? To get to the aji side. *

*(Aji is the Peruvian word for chilli)

A Jalapeño and his wife are sitting on the sofa when they hear a soft knocking at the door. 'Who could that be at this time of night?' says the wife. 'Go and see who it is.' The Jalapeño dutifully goes to the door and opens it, where he sees a Bird's Eye looking hopefully up at him. Without comment, the Jalapeño closes the door and sits down on the sofa. 'Well?' asks his wife and the Jalapeño replies, 'It's a little chilli outside'.

One chilli turns to the other and says, 'What time is it?' The other replies, 'I don't wear a watch, I habañero clue.'

Three chillies walk into a pub, looking slightly the worse for wear. The owner says 'Sorry lads, I can't serve you'. 'But why not?', slurs one of the chillies, steadying himself on the bar. The owner shakes his head sadly and replies, 'You've obviously been Cayenne-ing it all day.'

CHILLI HEAD QUIZ

So, now you've read the book you think you're an official Chilli Head. But woah, back up there young Chedi (chilli Jedi, geddit? Let's ignore the fact that Chedi is also the name of a Buddhist burial mound and a chain of 5-star hotels, shall we?) The heat is strong with you ('heat' is like the Chilli Head equivalent of the force, OK? Actually, this whole *Star Wars* thing isn't really working is it? But let's stick with it, it's nearly the end of the paragraph) but you must first pass the Chilli Head quiz before you become a true Chedi Master. Use the heat, Luke! (your name's probably not Luke is it? Look, do yourself a favour, just do the quiz and forget the whole Chedi thing, no one's going to be calling themselves that. Seriously).

 What is the name of the world's hottest chilli?
A. The Grim Reefer
B. Don't Fear the Reaper
C. Carolina Reaper

 Where was chilli con carne invented?
A. San Antonio
B. San Diego
C. Mexico City

 What is the name of the chemical in chillies that gives them their heat?
A. Cappuccino
B. Cap'n Crunch
C. Capsaicin

 Which country is the largest producer of raw chillies in the world?
A. US
B. China
C. India

5 What part of the chilli contains the most heat?
A. The skin
B. The seeds
C. The placental tissue

6 Where was the first ever chilli con carne cook-off held?
A. Terlingua, Texas
B. Fair Park, Dallas
C. Hatch Valley, New Mexico

7 The Guinness world record for eating the most Jalapeño peppers in one minute is currently held by Alfredo Hernandes. But how many did he eat?
A. 6
B. 16
C. 26

8 How many units does original Tabasco sauce rate on the Scoville scale?
A. 2.5–5K SHU
B. 25–50k SHU
C. 100–125K SHU

9 As of 2014, which chilli-driven fast food chain has the most outlets worldwide?
A. Chilli's
B. Nando's
C. Taco Bell

10 Which American President said 'Chili concocted outside of Texas is usually a weak, apologetic imitation of the real thing. One of the first things I do when I get home to Texas is to have a bowl of red. There is simply nothing better'?
A. George W. Bush
B. Abraham Lincoln
C. Lyndon B. Johnson

CHILLI HEAD DIRECTORY

ART
Chilli Thom chilithom.com *Chilli-inspired artworks*

CLOTHING
Cafe Press cafepress.com *Various*
High Seas Trading Co highseastrading.com *Various*
Hourglass Footwear hourglassfootwear.com *Sriracha-themed high heels*
Packer Shoes packershoes.com *Chilli trainers*

DRINK
Absinthes.com absinthes.com *Absinthe Red Chilli Head*
Fallen Angel Brewery fallenangelbrewery.com *Chilli beer*
Not On The High Street notonthehighstreet.com
  Make Your Own Organic Chilli Ginger Beer Kit

NOVELTY ITEMS
Amazon amazon.com and amazon.co.uk *Chilli-shaped salsa bowl, chilli party games, chilli magnet pens and chilli pinata*
Capsaicinoia chilligifts.co.uk *Chilli-themed novelty items*
Firebox firebox.com *Chilli party games*
Lakeland lakeland.co.uk *Chilli grinder*
MenKind menkind.co.uk *Ring of Fire After Curry Wipes*

SAUCES

Chilli Alchemist chillialchemist.co.uk
Peppers.com peppers.com
The Ribman theribman.co.uk

SEEDS

Chilli Pepper Company chileseeds.co.uk
Chilli Willy chilli-willy.com
Pucker Butt Pepper Company of South Carolina
   puckerbuttpeppercompany.com
Simpson's Seeds simpsonsseeds.co.uk
South Devon Chilli Farm southdevonchillifarm.co.uk

OTHER GARDENING SUPPLIES

Auto Pot autopot.co.uk *Self-watering systems for chilli plants*
LED Hydroponics ledhydroponics.co.uk *LED growing lights for*
   chilli plants

First published in the United Kingdom in 2015 by
Portico
1 Gower Street
London
WC1E 6HD

An imprint of Pavilion Books Company Ltd

ISBN 978-1-91023-203-3

A CIP catalogue record for this book is available from the British
Library.

10 9 8 7 6 5 4 3 2 1

Illustrations by Lee Hodges

Reproduction by Mission Productions Ltd, Hong Kong
Printed and bound by 1010 Printing International Ltd, China

This book can be ordered direct from the publisher at
www.pavilionbooks.com